RULING OVER THE EARTH

A Biblical View of Civil Government

Stephen McDowell

Providence Foundation

Ruling Over the Earth
A Biblical View of Civil Government

By Stephen McDowell

Published by:
Providence Foundation
PO Box 6759
Charlottesville, VA 22906
434-978-4535
Email: info@providencefoundation.com
www.providencefoundation.com

The Providence Foundation is a Christian educational organization whose purpose is to train leaders of education, business, and politics to transform their culture for Christ, and to teach all citizens how to disciple nations.

Cover painting: "Moses Elects the Council of Seventy Elders," painted by the Dutch artist Jacob de Wit in 1736-1737, hangs in the Rijksstudio Museum in Amsterdam. This painting, which was commissioned for the interior of the City Hall in Amsterdam, the Netherlands, reminds us that Israel was a representative republic with elected civil leaders.

ISBN: 978-1-887456-58-6
Printed in the United States of America

Table of Contents

Introduction

Our Biblical Duty to Learn about Government

The topic of civil government has been largely ignored by most of the evangelical community in the past century. Unlike in the previous centuries, especially during the founding era of America, it is rarely the topic of sermons. Many pastors avoid any talk of government and politics, whether from fear of offending church members or belief it is not their duty. They were not taught about government in seminary and, therefore, if they do address the issue, it is usually superficially, referencing the thirteenth chapter of the book of Romans saying we must obey the authorities and pay our taxes.

A majority of evangelical pastors believe that the Bible is sufficient to lead people to Christ and to teach them how to live a good moral life. However, it seems they do not believe the Bible is sufficient to teach God's people how to fulfill their original God-given mission to subdue and rule over the earth. More than 90% of theologically conservative pastors believe the Bible speaks to all areas of life and addresses specific civil issues facing Christians today (such as abortion, same-sex marriage, immigration, and so forth); yet only 10% of them are willing to address these issues. Because of this lack of teaching a practical biblical worldview, many Millennials see the church as irrelevant.[1]

Many reticent pastors and Christians do acknowledge that God is the ultimate governor and that no one rules except by God's authority, but then fail to say what we must do, other than to pray and have faith that God will prevail, if those who are governing reject the higher authority of God and rule according to their own worldview. After all, they say, the Bible really does not teach that we are to work to influence government but we are to be about the work of the kingdom, that is, converting souls.

Some pastors' approach to the topic of government centers on ethics. Some emphasize the attitudes we must have toward other believers who think differently than we do. Avoiding contention, strife, and divisions is certainly biblical and important and should be taught. Yet, it is equally important that pastors teach what the Bible says about government and civil duties. The church is to equip the saints for the works of service, including civil service (rendering to Caesar his due). It is to teach what the Bible says about all of life, including government. Without this instruction Christians will be ill equipped to act rightly and to "do justice" (Micah 6:8).

We need to be instructed in how to act biblically as well as in having correct attitudes. Varying views of church members is not a sufficient reason to avoid the subject. In fact, it is a reason why church leaders should seek out knowledge of the subject and teach the truth of God. God has one view on the subject of government, and His view is correct. Our task is to learn what the Bible says about this important subject so we can adopt His principles and obey His precepts, both personally and nationally.[2]

I have heard many Christians and pastors say that the Bible gives no specific form of government as the biblical ideal, that the Bible or Jesus did not present a certain kind of government that we are to seek to establish. It is true that there is no systematic teaching on the framework of biblical government. There is also no systematic teaching on many subjects, like the trinity, the doctrine of salvation, heaven, et cetera. Yet, the church has developed and teaches on these "religious" subjects with authority. Similarly we can and should study the principles that the Bible and Jesus teach regarding government for they have much to say on the subject, and, in fact, we will see that the Bible does present principles that support a particular kind of civil government as best.

Rev. Jonathan Mayhew, pastor of Boston's West Church, preached a sermon in 1750 entitled "A Discourse Concerning Unlimited Submission and Non-Resistance to the Higher Powers" which he knew some would think was "preaching politics, instead of Christ." He defended his action by citing 2 Timothy 3:16: "'All Scripture…is profitable for doctrine, for reproof, for correction, for instruction in righteousness.' Why, then, should not those parts of Scripture which relate to civil government be examined and explained from the desk, as well as others? Obedience to the civil magistrate is a Christian duty;

and if so, why should not the nature, grounds, and extent of it be considered in a Christian assembly?"

Mayhew begins his Discourse with the text of Romans 13:1-8, and then explains that civil government has "a moral and religious consideration," with a divine origin, and hence under the authority of God. He then says:

> although there be a sense, and a very plain and important sense, in which Christ's kingdom is not of this world [John 18:36], his inspired apostles have, nevertheless, laid down some general principles concerning the office of civil rulers, and the duty of subjects, together with the reason and obligation of that duty. And from hence it follows, that it is proper for all who acknowledge the authority of Jesus Christ, and the inspiration of his apostles, to endeavor to understand what is in fact the doctrine which they have delivered concerning this matter. It is the duty of Christian magistrates to inform themselves what it is which their religion teaches concerning the nature and design of their office. And it is equally the duty of all Christian people to inform themselves what it is which their religion teaches concerning that subjection which they owe to the higher powers.[3]

This book is a tool to assist you in fulfilling Mayhew's admonition of learning what the Bible teaches about the important subject of civil government. As those who are to equip the saints, pastors and church leaders must understand a biblical view of government and teach it to their members. To do less is to not only be disobedient, but to leave this important sphere in the hands of those who reject the authority of God and would establish man upon the throne as the source of all authority and law.

The Bible is authoritative in all it

A
DISCOURSE
CONCERNING
Unlimited Submiſſion
AND
Non-Reſiſtance
TO THE
HIGHER POWERS:
With ſome REFLECTIONS on the REſISTANCE made to
King CHARLES I.
AND ON THE
Anniversary of his Death:
In which the MYSTERIOUS Doctrine of that Prince's
Saintſhip and Martyrdom is UNRIDDLED:
The Subſtance of which was delivered in a SERMON preached in
the Weſt Meeting-Houſe in Boſton the LORD's-DAY after the
30th of January. 1749 | 50.

Publiſhed at the Requeſt of the Hearers.

By JONATHAN MAYHEW, A. M.
Paſtor of the Weſt Church in Boſton.

Jonathan Mayhew's sermon.

says,[4] and the Bible speaks to all of life. It most certainly gives us much information about that earthly government that has the power to affect every area of our lives. We should fulfill our duty to learn what the Bible says about government, teach it to others, and live out its implications every day.

Chapter 1

What Is Government?

God is the ultimate source of all power and authority (John 19:11; Rom. 13:1; Rev. 1:5). He is the ultimate governor of all His creation (Dan. 4:17, 25-26, 31-32, 35; Ps. 22:28). The very first verse in the Bible establishes this important truth: "In the beginning God created the heaven and the earth" (Gen. 1:1). As Creator He has dominion over all things. Acts 17:24-28 affirms this and other important ideas regarding government:

> The God who made the world and all things in it, since He is Lord of heaven and earth, does not dwell in temples made with hands; neither is He served by human hands, as though He needed anything, since He Himself gives to all life and breath and all things; and He made from one, every nation of mankind to live on all the face of the earth, having determined their appointed times, and the boundaries of their habitation, that they should seek God, if perhaps they might grope for Him and find Him, though He is not far from each one of us; for in Him we live and move and exist.

From this and other Scriptures we learn four foundational doctrines that underlie a correct understanding of government. These are:

1. Creation – God created all things (Acts 17:24; Gen. 1:1; Heb. 11:3; Ps. 33:6; Jer. 51:15).
2. Lordship – God is Lord over all His creation (Acts 17:24; Isa. 40; 1 Tim. 1:17; 6:15; Ps. 47: 2-3, 7-8; Zech. 14:9; Rev. 19:16).
3. Providence—God sustains all things (Acts 17: 25, 28; Col. 1:15-17; Job 34:14-15; 1 Tim. 6:13).
4. Sovereignty – God governs all (Acts 17:26; Dan. 4:17, 25-26, 32; Dan. 2:21; Ps. 103:19; Ps. 115:3; Ps. 135:6; Ps. 22:28; Isa. 9:6-7).

God not only created all things, but He also sustains and governs all things via His laws and active involvement in His creation. Nothing is outside His plan and governance. Nothing in the universe is autonomous; that is, nothing has self-rule (although fallen, sinful man seeks to do so). This is God's world which is governed by God's laws, and men violate them to their own harm.

While God is the ultimate governor of His creation, He has given man the commission to rule over His earth (Gen. 1:26-28). God governs according to His law, and since He requires civil leaders to administer His justice (that is, His law), any discussion of biblical civil government necessitates discussion of how His law applies to mankind in the civil arena. It is beyond the scope of this work to explore this topic in great detail. The author does so in other works.[5] Many writers have addressed this topic as well.[6] While we will touch on some application of God's Word regarding the laws of nations, we will largely explore the broader topic of civil government.

Origin of Civil Government

The history of government begins in the Garden of Eden with the first man. God placed man in the Garden and gave him a dominion mandate to subdue and rule all creatures, which included man governing himself.

> Then God said: "Let Us make man in Our image…and let them rule."…male and female He created them…God said to them, "Be fruitful and multiply, and fill the earth, and subdue it; and rule …over every living thing that moves on the earth." - Gen. 1:26-28

God created everything and so everything belongs to Him and is under His domain. The earth is the Lord's and all it contains (Gen. 1-2; Ex. 9:29; 19:5; Dt. 10:14; Lev. 25:23; 1 Chron. 29:11; Job 41:11; Ps. 24:1; 50:10-12; 1 Cor. 10:26). Yet, God has given to man the authority to rule over the earth. "The heavens are the heavens of the Lord; but the earth He has given to the sons of men" (Psalm 115:16).

Ruling Over the Earth

God gave man the task of ruling over the earth, of being God's steward over the earth. He was God's delegated ruler over the earth, and as such he was to rule in accordance with God's truth and under God's direction. Psalm 8 affirms man's calling to rule: "Thou dost make him to rule over the works of

Thy hands; Thou hast put all things under his feet" (v. 6). And Paul writes that Christians are to judge matters of this life (1 Cor. 6:3).

All government, therefore, begins with the individual. Power flows from the individual to the other spheres of life. The test of man's self-government in the beginning was his ability to resist eating of the forbidden tree without any type of external restraints. He had to internally govern himself according to God's Creation Law in order to succeed (Genesis 2:16-17).

Creation Law is also known as the "Law of Nature" (Romans 1:18-20; 2:14-15). The Law of Nature was supplemented later by the "Law of Nature's God," i.e. the revealed Law of God in the Bible. The Law of Nature is summed up succinctly in the Golden Rule (do unto others as you would have others do unto you, Matt 7:12) and in the command to "love your neighbor as yourself" (Gal 5:14). The Moral Law (Creation Law) was originally written in the heart of man, but after the fall man could no longer clearly discern God's law. God mercifully gave man His Law in written form so he could more clearly see and pass on God's liberating truth.

Through Adam's failure to control himself, sin entered into the world and made it difficult for any man to govern himself. At this time no civil government had been established as God intended for man to be self-governed with no need for external restraints. He had created the family where government was exercised, but it was limited in jurisdiction. The dominion mandate initially given to Adam and Eve (the family) did not include the responsibility for ruling over other men. Therefore, when Cain did not control his anger and jealousy, and he violently slew his brother, God Himself took responsibility for justice and protection (Genesis 4:1-16).

After a period of time the prevalence of sin and lack of self-government led to so much violence that God saw the end result would be all men destroying one another (Genesis 6:5-13). Therefore, God decided to intervene and bring a flood to destroy all but one righteous family. When God brought Noah through the flood to a new earth, He re-established the cultural mandate, but modified it by delegating to man the responsibility for governing other men in order to protect innocent human life from sinful, violent men (Gen 9:5-7). He does this by instituting capital punishment, the backbone of civil government – "whoever sheds man's blood, by man his blood shall be shed" (v. 6).[7] Thus civil government began as a divine institution designed by God to protect life and provide a peaceful environment in which man could fulfill the cultural mandate.

Definition of Government

Self and Civil Government

All earthly government begins in the heart of man with his ability (or inability) to direct, regulate, manage, and control his life. God created man with the capacity for total self-government. When he fell and lost this capacity, God instituted civil government for our well-being.

When people hear the word government they usually think of civil government, for in most nations that is the ultimate government. In a general sense, *government* means direction, regulation, control, restraint.[8] There are many spheres of government with each providing direction, regulation, control, and restraint in its jurisdiction. The spheres of government can be divided into internal and external government. Another name for internal government is self-government. All government begins internally in the heart of man, with his ability to govern his conscience, will, character, thoughts, ideas, motives, convictions, attitudes, and desires. How a man governs himself internally affects his external actions, speech, conduct, use of property, and many other things. Each external sphere of government is a reflection of the internal sphere. In other words, the internal is causative to the external. The type of government that exists in the homes, churches, schools, businesses, associations, or civil realms of a country is a reflection of the self-government, or lack of self-government, within the citizens. The following diagram depicts this idea of government.

Internal Government ⟶ External Government

Self

Family
Church
School
Business / Vocation / Work
Associations
Civil

The seventeenth century Dutch scholar, Hugo Grotius, who systematized the subject of the law of nations, summarized the principle of self-government, writing:

He knows not how to rule a kingdom, that cannot manage a Province; nor can he wield a Province, that cannot order a City; nor he order a City, that knows not how to regulate a Village; nor he a Village, that cannot guide a Family; nor can that man Govern well a Family that knows not how to Govern himself; neither can any Govern himself unless his reason be Lord, Will and Appetite her Vassals; nor can Reason rule unless herself be ruled by God, and (wholly) be obedient to Him.[9]

Hugo Grotius

Stated another way, you must rule yourself before you can rule others. Paul and other biblical authors admonished us to be self-controlled (Gal. 5:23; 1 Thess. 5:6; Tit. 1:8; 1 Pet. 5:8). The Bible teaches that rulers must be self-governed. One quality of a church leader was that he "manages his own household well, keeping his children under control with all dignity (but if a man does not know how to manage his own household, how will he take care of the church of God?)" (1 Timothy 3:4-5).

There are many civil government leaders today who are attempting to govern their nation, yet are unable to effectively direct and control their own lives or their families. These men and women should be replaced by those who can rule their own lives. Those who are self-governed are the ones with real power according to the Bible: "He who is slow to anger is better than the mighty, and he who rules his spirit, than he who captures a city" (Prov. 16:32).

Grotius' statement reveals how the flow of power should occur within a country, from the internal to the external. He speaks of decentralized governmental units wielding less power the further removed they are from the individual. The following chart summarizes his ideas.

Spheres of Government

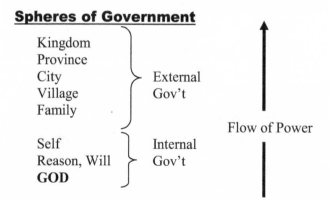

Kingdom
Province
City   External
Village   Gov't
Family

                                        Flow of Power

Self   Internal
Reason, Will   Gov't
GOD

Effective government begins by an individual learning to govern himself. The more internal self-government a person possesses the less external government he needs. Consequently, the more rules and laws required to keep people acting rightly is a revelation of a diminishing amount of self-government.[10] History teaches that man can control himself, but only to a limited degree. Since self-government cannot be imposed externally, and man is limited in personal self-discipline, there must be another source for internal control. Grotius reveals that man can only be truly self-governed if his reason, will, and appetite are ruled by God. The basis of self-control is obedience to the Creator and His standards of conduct found in the Bible. Robert C. Winthrop, speaker of the U.S. House of Representatives from 1847-49, said in 1849:

> All societies of men must be governed in some way or other. The less they may have of stringent State Government, the more they must have of individual self-government. The less they rely on public law or physical force, the more they must rely on private moral restraint. Men, in a word, must necessarily be controlled either by a power within them, or by a power without them; either by the Word of God, or by the strong arm of man; either by the Bible or the bayonet.[11]

Robert C. Winthrop

Winthrop summarized well the operation of government in the earth for all men and nations throughout all history: all men will be governed, ultimately "either by the Word of God, or by the strong arm of man; either by the Bible or the bayonet."

Self-government is limited apart from God; therefore, the ability to govern well is limited where the people and leaders do not seek to govern themselves and their nation under God. George Washington said, "It is impossible to govern the universe without the aid of a Supreme Being."[12]

George Washington

The foundation for self-government is laid in the families of a nation. Noah Webster wrote in *A Manual of Useful Studies:*

In the family are formed the elements of civil government; the family discipline is the model of all social order; ... the respect for the law and the magistrate begins in the respect for parents.... Families are the nurseries of good and bad citizens. The parent who neglects to restrain and govern his child, or who, by his example, corrupts him, is the enemy of the community to which he belongs; the parent who instructs his child in good principles, and subjects him to correct discipline, is the guardian angel of his child, and the best benefactor of society.[13]

Noah Webster

As people in a nation become less self-governed, and give up power, the civil government (especially the national government) will grow and grow, making more and more laws (many outside its realm of jurisdiction) and spending more and more money. Lack of self-government leads to greater centralized external government which results in loss of individual liberty.

The problems and failures of our civil government are due to the declining ability of individuals to properly direct their own affairs, which has arisen as families, churches, and schools have abandoned their biblical duty. The solution rests with the family, and other educational institutions, implanting within Americans self-government and other vital Christian principles.

Other Spheres of Government

As mentioned above, there are various spheres of government, each playing an important role in life and God's intended societal structure. Examining these in detail is beyond the scope of this work, but a brief statement of each governmental sphere follows.

Family Government

The family is a divine institution and the basic building block of society. It is man's first school, first church, first business, and first state. It shapes one's view of life. You are first governed in a family, but then you begin to govern as you establish your family. God created the family in the beginning as the means for accomplishing His mission for mankind to be fruitful, to multiply, and to rule over the earth. The family is God's chief instrument of biblical transformation. It is God's primary tool for extending His kingdom – His government – in the earth. As the family goes, so goes the nation.[14]

The family is the primary institution in the earth because it is a creation ordinance. The other two divine institutions (the church and civil government) originated after the fall of mankind to assist fallen man to recapture for God His earth and fulfill the original dominion mandate. The family is of such importance that three of the Ten Commandments (5, 7, and 10) protect it.

Under biblical law the husband and wife are considered one person with both benefitting from its provisions and protections. God commanded Israel, and all men, to honor their fathers and mothers. Both father and mother are to be honored equally. When this commandment was given to Israel, no nation in the world provided such esteem to mothers.

While there is equality of men and women under God's law, it does not favor the manhood of woman. God created man as male and female in the beginning, and each has unique characteristics and callings. They both are to fulfill the cultural mandate, but they have different roles in doing so. God gave man greater physical strength and endurance to till the ground, cultivate mechanical arts, and, if necessary, fight to preserve life, liberty, and property. While women are capable managers of business and non-domestic affairs (see Proverbs 31), their first responsibility is to see that the home is an instrument of godly transformation. They are to provide an environment of light and joy, where children are nourished and trained to advance God's kingdom in all spheres of life and pass on to posterity principles of liberty.

The foundation for self-government is laid in the families of a nation. Families must begin early teaching the principle of self-government. One night, many years ago I was teaching my son, who was then about six years old, about self-government. I gave him a definition he could understand, telling him that "self-government is doing what you are supposed to do without anybody telling you." The next morning he woke me early, took me to his bedroom, pointed to his bed, which he had made up all by himself without anybody telling him to do so, and remarked: "Dad, I was being self-governed, wasn't I?" The transformation of nations begins with such small steps.

Church Government

The church and its leaders are to build up and equip believers to fulfill the calling of God upon their lives and to accomplish His overall purposes in the earth (Eph. 4:11-13). The church prepares people to govern society (to rule, Ps. 8:6) and to fulfill the redemption and creation commissions. It does this by providing regular instruction in biblical truth for every sphere of life (Mt. 28:18-20, 2 Tim. 3:16-17), administering sacraments and church discipline (1 Cor. 5:8-13; 11:23-25; Mt. 18:15-17), and discipling, equipping, and organizing believers (Eph. 4:11-12, 16; Titus 3:8, 14).

God gives the church and its leaders authority to accomplish its mission. Government operates within the institution, and God gives direction in the Scriptures regarding the structure of church government.[15]

A statement by David Gregg describing the early American Republic states well the role of the church in a Christian nation: "The people made the laws, and the churches made the people."[16] The role of the church is not to directly hold power as an ecclesiastical body that makes civil law. The influence of the church on government is not by positional power, but by the influential power of its teachings.

School

The role of the school in a nation should simply be an extension of the educational role of the home. Where there are Christian homes, there will be Christian schools, assuming there is freedom to establish schools. If there is no freedom, the rise in Christian homes will produce men of character and wisdom who will work to change the government and laws which will then allow freedom to educate in a biblical manner.

Education has an important role in society. Teaching biblical truth is how we will disciple the nations (Matt. 28:18-20). We must keep the right and responsibility of educating children in the hands of parents. If we surrender it to the state we have surrendered our self-government.

Vocation / Work / Business

Government exists within the workplace. The best workers are those who govern themselves and diligently fulfill their function within the workplace. Work in general is a vital part of God's mission for us in the earth. It is a primary way we take dominion over the earth. We provide needed goods or services through our work. We are to govern our work in accordance with God's Word. Our work is an important part of our calling.[17]

Associations

As we voluntarily work with others in Christian union we will be able to more effectively accomplish our mission in the earth. Hence, we can form various associations to help the poor, preach the gospel, educate the ignorant, et cetera.

Civil

As has been stated, civil government is a divine institution given certain delegated powers by God so it can accomplish an important but limited function in God's overall plan for mankind.

While there are many spheres of government, these are not all divine institutions. God created three divine institutions – family, church, and state – out of which these spheres of government flow (see Chapter 6 for more). The Bible gives guidelines for the unique form of government each of these divine institutions have. More on the structure of biblical civil government follows.

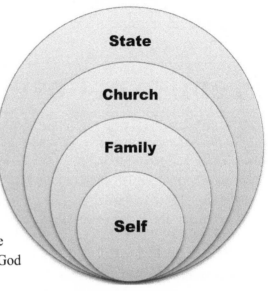

Effective government in every sphere of life begins by an individual learning to govern himself.

Chapter 2

Premise of Government

To understand the role of government we must understand two important ideas. One, man is sinful and his heart is deceitful and desperately wicked; consequently, he tends to abuse power. Two, God wants mankind to live in great liberty. These two ideas provide a framework for us as we consider the purpose, power, form, and scope of government.

1. Since man is sinful and his heart is desperately wicked, he tends to abuse power.

The Bible teaches that man was created in the image of God (Gen. 1: 26), communed with Him, and had the capacity to obey Him completely (Gen. 1-2). Yet man disobeyed God (i.e. he sinned), which separated him from God and corrupted his heart (Gen. 3; Rom. 3:9-18, 23). Thus after man sinned his nature changed, from having an obedient pure heart toward God to having a rebellious evil heart – as the Bible informs us, "the intent of man's heart is evil from his youth" (Gen. 8:21).

Since "every intent of the thoughts of his heart was only evil continually" (Gen. 6:5), "the earth was filled with violence" (vs. 11). The external violence that flowed out of man's evil, sinful heart was so bad that God sent a flood to wipe out all but eight people, with whom he started anew. Yet even so, man remained in a fallen, sinful condition. His heart remained darkened. Jeremiah explains: "the heart is deceitful above all things, and desperately wicked" (Jer. 17:9, KJV).

God established civil government after man fell as a means of protecting life, punishing evil-doers, and executing His justice (Gen. 9:6: Rom. 13:1-7). Civil government is a divine institution, as much so as is the family and the church. Unlike the family, it was not established at creation but rather after the fall of man.

Ever since the fall, man is born in sin and is unclean (Job 14:4; Ps. 51:5). He has a darkened heart (Rom. 1:21). This biblical truth reveals the primary reason why men commit evil acts.[18] Man's sinful and deceitful heart produces all kinds of evil actions. The Bible says wars, fights, quarrels, and murders occur due to sin, envy, selfishness, and lust (James 4:1-2; Matt. 15:19).

Seeing man as sinful will affect how we live and conduct our societal affairs. One consequence is that we will not entrust man with too much power, because sinful man will tend to abuse power. President John Adams said:

> To expect self-denial from men, when they have a majority in their favor, and consequently power to gratify themselves, is to disbelieve all history and universal experience; it is to disbelieve Revelation and the Word of God, which informs us, the heart is deceitful above all things, and desperately wicked.... There is no man so blind as not to see, that to talk of founding a government upon a supposition that nations and great bodies of men, left to themselves, will practice a course of self-denial, is either to babble like a new-born infant, or to deceive like an unprincipled impostor.[19]

John Adams

We seek to limit the power of our rulers in various ways: binding them down with a constitution; holding them accountable with frequent elections; dividing the legislative, executive, and judicial powers; and setting up checks and balances within these separate governing bodies. Thus, a people's view of man affects the form of civil government they adopt. It also affects their execution of justice, which should be swift but fair.

James Madison wrote in the Federalist: "If men were angels, no government would be necessary."[20] However, the Bible teaches men are not angels, but fallen and fallible beings who have a sinful nature and, thus, cannot be entrusted with too much power. God knew this when he set up the unique government of ancient Israel. (The structure of the government of ancient Israel is examined in Chapter 8.) Any nation desiring to live in liberty should seek to incorporate biblical structures of government.

2. God wants mankind to live in great liberty.

A central theme of the Bible is the liberation of mankind. As we live out our Christian faith in the earth, we must understand the nature of this liberty and construct governments that secure this God-given liberty.

God delivered Israel from slavery, and He gave them laws that made them free men. The principles in the Ten Commandments produce religious, civil, and economic liberty for all men.

Jesus came to liberate man: "It was for freedom that Christ came to set us free" (Gal. 5:1). In what could be called Jesus' inaugural address (Luke 4:18-19), He tells us that He was sent to proclaim release to the captives and to set at liberty those who are oppressed. Jesus manifested the kingdom of God by liberating man — physically, mentally, and spiritually — and casting out Satan and his cohorts, who seek only to destroy and bring man into bondage.

Jesus gave us His Spirit so that we might live free because, "Where the Spirit of the Lord is, there is liberty" (2 Corinthians 3:17). When the Spirit of the Lord comes into the heart of a man, that man is liberated. Likewise, when the Spirit of the Lord comes into a nation, that nation is liberated. The degree to which the Spirit of the Lord is infused into a society (through its people, laws, and institutions) is the degree to which that society will experience liberty in every realm (personal, political, civil, religious, and economic). Spiritual freedom ultimately produces political freedom. External political slavery reflects internal spiritual bondage.

Jesus came to set us free, both internally and externally. He gave us internal freedom from the bondage of sin as well as external freedom from the fruit of sin in the earth. He came to give us both personal and civil freedom. He came to not only bring internal personal salvation, but also external political freedom. Christ Jesus provided God's pathway to liberty for man, which is from the internal to the external.

In Acts 1:6 Jesus' disciples asked Him when the kingdom of God would be restored. They were thinking of an external kingdom. They thought the Messiah would set up such a kingdom and deliver them from external bondage. How did Jesus respond to this question? He did not deny that the kingdom would be manifested externally on the earth. He said that times and epochs would follow that would contribute to bringing God's rule and reign on the earth (see Acts 1:7-8). We can look back over the centuries and see those times and epochs. Since the time of Christ there has been no end to the increase of His government or kingdom in the earth (Luke 1:33) — it has grown steadily. But Jesus did correct their wrong understanding of how the kingdom would come. He said it would first be birthed within man's heart (the kingdom of God is within you, Luke 17:20-21) which would then flow out from him and affect every sphere of life.

God's plan is to bring liberty to man — internal and external, spiritual and physical, personal and civil liberty. God is the author of liberty, all liberty. Engraved on the memorial in Washington, DC, honoring Thomas Jefferson are his words: "God who gave us life gave us liberty. Can the liberties of a nation be secure when we have removed a conviction that these liberties are the gift of God?" America's Founders

Engraved on the Jefferson Memorial are his words: "God who gave us life gave us liberty. Can the liberties of a nation be secure when we have removed a conviction that these liberties are the gift of God?"

knew, in the words of Jefferson's pastor Rev. Charles Clay, that "the sacred cause of liberty [is] the cause of God."[21] John Dickinson, a signer of the Constitution, wrote, "Our cause ... is nothing less, than to maintain the Liberty with which heav'n itself hath made us free."[22]

John Dickinson

Historian of the American Revolution, David Ramsay, said: "There can be no political happiness, without liberty; there can be no liberty without morality; and there can be no morality, without religion."[23] When our Founders spoke of religion, they meant Christianity, for Christianity was true religion to them. Noah Webster wrote in his United States history textbook:

Almost all the civil liberty now enjoyed in the world owes its origin to the principles of the Christian religion.... The religion which has introduced civil liberty, is the religion of Christ and his apostles, which enjoins humility, piety, and benevolence; which acknowledges in every person a brother, or a sister, and a citizen with equal rights. This is genuine Christianity, and to this we owe our free constitutions of government.[24]

We need to understand the great liberty that God desires us to have. Lack of knowledge of the value and source of our liberty has caused many people today, including many Christians, to give up their liberty for a little security and care. Like Esau, these people have traded their birthright for a bowl of pottage.

Through Christ's liberating work, we can be freed to direct our own affairs under God. Even God Himself does not seek to control us from without, but wants us to desire to obey Him from within. His kingdom is birthed within us, where we consent to live in it. God does judge the acts of every man, but He does not control all the actions of men. Jesus gave to the state what it can take by force — money (via taxes), material things, and even His physical life (for a time) — but He never gave His freedom, His self-determination to accomplish His purpose, or His belief in His Father.

Many have given to Caesar (the state) the control of their lives (or at least part of their lives) thinking that government or leaders should control them and/or provide for them. We are not to render to Caesar our liberty, our self-determination, or our care. We become slaves if we do so. God created man and desires redeemed man to live free under Him, to act and make choices, to labor and be productive, to take dominion. He delegated to us the responsibility to govern our destiny, our children, and our property.

Throughout history many people have resigned themselves to the idea that their lot in life is already determined and they can do little about it. Two examples include the Hindu caste system and the feudal system where some were peasants and laborers, some lords, some knights. People in these instances surrender to the idea that other people or circumstances govern who they are, what they will do, and where they will be. The Christian idea of man and the Christian idea of history declare something different. God says we can change things. If society contains evil, then we can and should change it. If something is wrong in our life, we can change it by God's grace. We can be changed, and we can change society because we have access to God, His truth, and His liberty. He tells us to continually grow into His image.

God wants us to live free under Him, directing our own affairs, in covenant with others, fulfilling His purposes for our lives. Others, via government or force, are not to direct our lives or tell us everything to do (from how to educate our children to what food to eat, to how to spend our money, or how to support the poor). We are not to give to the state control of our lives, liberty, or property; nor are we to look to government to provide our needs, manage our affairs, or fulfill our responsibilities.

God does not intend for earthly authorities to control us. We are to govern ourselves under God and His standard of truth. We should seek to change the mentality of letting others govern. Civil government is supposed to restrict unlawful behavior of men who would take or threaten the life, liberty, and property of others. It wields the sword for this reason (Romans 13:4). It controls evil men, but not those who do what is right.

Freedom to choose is one key way we resemble God. As we choose what pleases Him, we bring Him glory. When evil governments (or other evil men) deprive us of the ability to make free choices, a part of our God-likeness is suppressed. Thus people will pay almost any price for freedom. Patrick Henry's cry, "Give me liberty or give me death!" resonates deep in the heart of all men created in God's image.[25]

Chapter 3

Biblical Doctrine of Government in Romans 13

Paul's writing in Romans 13 is perhaps the best known passage of Scripture regarding civil government. He presents a clear overview of the doctrine of government in the first seven verses, showing that we are to be subject to lawful authority in attitude and action.

[1] Every person is to be in subjection to the governing authorities. For there is no authority except from God, and those which exist are established by God. [2] Therefore whoever resists authority has opposed the ordinance of God; and they who have opposed will receive condemnation upon themselves. [3] For rulers are not a cause of fear for good behavior, but for evil. Do you want to have no fear of authority? Do what is good and you will have praise from the same; [4] for it is a minister of God to you for good. But if you do what is evil, be afraid; for it does not bear the sword for nothing; for it is a minister of God, an avenger who brings wrath on the one who practices evil. [5] Therefore it is necessary to be in subjection, not only because of wrath, but also for conscience' sake. [6] For because of this you also pay taxes, for rulers are servants of God, devoting themselves to this very thing. [7] Render to all what is due them: tax to whom tax is due; custom to whom custom; fear to whom fear; honor to whom honor. (Romans 13:1-7, NASB)

Some of the principles taught in this passage of Scripture include:

1. Civil government is a divine institution ordained by God. All authority is from God.

We examined the origin of civil government in the book of Genesis above. God established government after the fall of mankind to deal with the sinful actions of men. Civil government is a part of God's kingdom and government, and is itself subject to God. "Every person is to be in subjection to the governing authorities," which includes those who govern. They are not above the law. Everyone, including governing officials, are subject to the Highest Authority, God.

Civil government's authority is delegated to it by God, just as is the authority of parents and church leaders. God is the source of all lawful authority. Commenting on Romans 13:1, theologian Charles Hodge wrote,

> All authority is of God. No man has any rightful power over other men, which is not derived from God. All human power is delegated and ministerial. This is true of parents, of magistrates, and of church officers. This, however, is not all the passage means. It not only asserts that all government …is…derived from God, but that every magistrate is of God; that is, his authority is *jure divino [divine right]*.[26]

Every official, no matter how he assumes his office and what type of government he operates within, has been delegated authority from God to fulfill the godly mission of government to be "an avenger who brings wrath on the one who practices evil" and to be a minister "to you for good." All civil leaders are to be ministers of God's justice, although all do not do so. All have the same duty, yet all do not fulfill that duty. If civil government fulfills its duty, we have an obligation to obey and support it.

Authorities are established (ordained, appointed) by God; that is, they rule only as He allows it. But this does not mean that He arbitrarily appoints all rulers for all nations because the Bible also teaches that those who rule reflect the type of government that the people deserve. God allows the sowing and reaping process to take place in the type of leaders we have. Israel chose their rulers of tens, fifties, hundreds, and thousands (Deut. 1:13; Ex. 18:21-22). They consented to whom would be king (2 Sam. 2:4; 5:1-3; 1 Chron. 11:3). Therefore, when Paul speaks of appointment, this does not usually mean direct selection by God.

All authority and power is from God. By Him kings reign (Prov. 8:15). The usurpation or abuse of power by rulers is not of God, but the power itself is.

Even the most corrupt rulers' power is from God (John 19:11). Magistrates bear the image of God's authority. Even bad governments perform some good function of providing a degree of order or peace (consider for example, some Middle Eastern nations under current monarchs, or former rulers like Saddam Hussein). Magistrates are God's servants. They will give account to Him one day on how they governed.

2. God established civil government for the good of man. It is to be a minister (servant) of God for good.

Paul teaches that civil government was instituted by God for the good of mankind. Government is not intrinsically evil. It was not created to be our enemy but for our good. However, to function in this manner, it must perform its biblical purpose. All of God's creation is good, but God's good creation can be used for evil when not used according to His specifications in His Word (abuse of plants via drugs or drunkenness is one of innumerable examples).

God ordained government for the good of mankind, but man can and has used it for evil. As expressed previously, this is because man is fallen and sinful and his heart is desperately wicked. When placed in positions of power, his tendency is to abuse that power, as witnessed throughout history.

In the context of his teaching on government Paul tells us that we are to overcome evil in the heart of man by the truth of the Gospel (Romans 12). He then writes we are to overcome evil in society by godly civil government (Romans 13:1-4).

Civil government represents God, not the people. It is His servant. It must execute God's justice, not what it considers to be good for the people. It must look to the only One who is good, God, to be able to

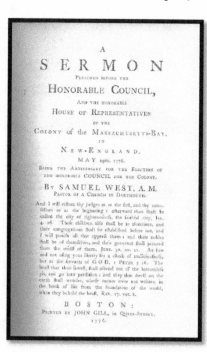

An Election Sermon preached by Samuel West, May 29th, 1776

administer good (that which is just and right). Rulers are to be servants of God, but they are also to be servants of men rather than lording it over them. (Jesus taught this in Luke 25; see Chapter 5.)

For rulers to best fulfill their biblical mandate as ministers of God for good, we need good people governing. Hence, we must work to get good people in government.

In an election sermon preached in 1776 before the government leaders of Massachusetts, Rev. Samuel West said:

> Magistrates are ministers of God.... [W]henever they pursue measures directly destructive of the public good they cease being God's ministers, they forfeit their right to obedience from the subject, they become pests of society, and the community is under the strongest obligation of duty, both to God and to its own members, to resist and oppose them, which will be so far from resisting the ordinance of God that it will be strictly obeying his commands.[27]

3. Everyone is to be in subjection to governing authorities. We are to resist those who rebel against God's higher law.

We are "to be in subjection to the governing authorities" (v. 1, 5). We are not necessarily to obey every mandate of government. When Paul writes that resistance to authority equals resistance to God, he is not presenting an unqualified statement of unlimited submission to all civil authorities because we see in the book of Acts that the apostles resisted governing authorities (Acts 4:18-20; 5:17-29; 16:35-40). The Hebrew midwives, Daniel, and many other Old Testament saints disobeyed the commands of Pharaohs and kings (see for example, Ex. 1:15 - 2:3; Dan. 3, 6). The Bible teaches we must obey God rather than man (Acts 5:29). So we are at times to resist the higher authority and obey the Highest authority (God). We are to render to civil rulers what is due them (v. 7), not more than what is due them. Colonial minister Jonathan Mayhew addressed this well in his sermon, "A Discourse Concerning Unlimited Submission and Non-Resistance to the Higher Powers," preached in Boston in 1750.[28]

There is no unlimited submission to civil authorities. After all, Jesus is Lord, not Caesar. Throughout history "Caesars" – that is, civil leaders – have often claimed to be the ultimate authority, denying in word and action the true Lord of all heaven and earth.

Charles Hodge explains Paul's object in these passages is that,

> Magistrates are to be obeyed. The extent of this obedience is to be determined from the nature of the case. They are to be obeyed as magistrates, in the exercise of their lawful authority. When Paul commands wives to obey their husbands, they are required to obey them as husbands, not as masters, nor as kings; children are to obey their parents as parents, not as sovereigns; and so in every case.[29]

Therefore, to obey the state if it attempts to perform functions of the church or family is to disobey God and render to Caesar the things that are God's. (We will examine more on this important civil teaching of Jesus Christ in Chapter 5.)

The context of "subjection to governing authorities" in verses 1-5 is rulers who do good and not evil. If rulers do evil, we must act appropriately by obeying God and seeking to change evil government (following the biblical steps of how to resist the tyrant, which will be discussed in Chapter 5). Rulers are to minister good and execute God's justice against evil. If they do, then

The Hebrew midwives disobeyed the command of Pharaoh yet obeyed the command of God.

we are to obey them, but we are not to support them if they administer evil. How we withhold support from evil rulers will be discussed later.

All power is ordained by God, and civil leaders have a duty to administer God's justice. We are to obey them as civil rulers fulfilling this purpose. We do not obey them as God, unconditionally.

4. Civil government has been given authority to use force (the sword) to deal with evil doers.

Civil government is God's instrument "who brings wrath on the one who practices evil." It has been given authority to use force – "it does not bear the sword for nothing" – to execute God's vengeance upon evil doers, upon those who break God's civil laws. As individuals, we are not to execute vengeance upon evil doers, or take revenge (Rom. 12:17, 19). We are to love our enemies (Matt. 5:44) and overcome evil with good (Rom. 12:21). Government is God's instrument to execute His justice in the earth. Evil action of men is to be overcome by good government.

God gives civil government the authority to use force. It is not given to individuals or the family or church; although, each of these entities have illegitimately used force in various societies throughout history to execute what they considered to be justice. The Bible provides guidelines for the proportion and type of force, as well as for the criminal penalties for various crimes.[30]

Rulers are to restrain and punish evil men, not good men. If they punish good men they are operating outside their domain, and hence, outside this Scriptural command. As such we are under no obligation to obey. When we "do what is good," we should not be in fear of government. Government should praise us. If government condemns us and inflicts fear upon us when we do what is good, it is operating illegitimately. When vile men rule, government is a terror (Ps. 12:1, 8). Rulers are to be a terror to evil-doers. However, they are often a terror to good-doers. If so, we have a responsibility to take all appropriate actions to change this.

While vile government can provide some protection to people – for example, while some of the leaders of Rome suppressed various God-given rights of people in the empire, they did provide some degree of peace, order, and justice – only godly government will provide the security and blessings that God intends for mankind.

Rulers are to bear the sword of war and the sword of justice. Due to the sinful nature of man, he will not always restrain himself from evil by his own inward convictions or conscience (although Paul says that even sinful man is governed to some degree by his conscience, see Romans 1 and 2). Therefore, the fear of punishment will provide a restraint to sinful people. God's laws and their penalties help restrain evil-doers (1 Tim. 1:9); therefore, the laws of a nation should be based upon God's law to be most effective at restraining evil. God's penalties best deter fallen men from evil actions.[31]

When rulers punish evil men they act as God's servants, because God wants peace and order (1 Tim. 2), which are best instituted when rulers uphold His laws and penalties. They are God's ministers bringing judgment on the action of men. They are not to punish men for wrong intentions and thoughts. Only God judges thoughts and intents.

5. Biblical civil government will not violate Christian conscience.

Romans 13:5 says, "Therefore it is necessary to be in subjection, not only because of wrath, but also for conscience' sake." Our conscience tells us what is right to do; that is, it tells us to obey God. Therefore, if government is commanding action contrary to God, our conscience will not tell us to obey evil government, but rather God's law. Subjection requires our submission to government; that is, we place ourselves under someone else. But when government requires something of us that is contrary to God's word, we must obey God rather than man (Acts 5:29). Even here, we are submissive, in the sense that we will realize that there will be consequences for disobeying leaders. When do we disobey government? When it forbids what God commands (like prayer, Daniel 6) or commands what God forbids (like idolatry, Daniel 3).

To be in subjection "for conscience' sake" does not mean that we are to subject our conscience to the will of government leaders or to any man. Only God can make laws binding our conscience. We are to render to God what belongs to God, and our conscience belongs to God, not man. However, pagan man will attempt to govern the conscience. Today, secularists are enacting laws punishing those who oppose homosexuality, attempting to force many businessmen to violate their conscience. They pass hate laws thinking they can discern the motives of the heart.

God wants our subjection to be voluntary and sincere (Eccl. 10:20; 1 Pet. 2:17), but if the ruler's laws violate God's law then this cannot be. Secular governments will enact laws that violate some aspect of God's law. We must resist such tyrannical rulers (see Chapter 5 for how to do this), while at the same time seek to establish godly government. As we take steps to resist and evaluate the probability of success we exhibit "a patient subjection to the penalty without resistance."[32] The first century church had little hope of changing unlawful authority and so having this attitude and action showed the rightness of the Christian faith. If we resist unbiblical civil laws, the wrath of civil government will come upon us. We must be prepared to suffer the consequences. But if we subject ourselves to unbiblical laws for fear of punishment, then God will deal with us for disobedience.

We are to be subject to our government and its laws not just out of fear of punishment but for conscience sake. But this requires that the laws that we obey are not in violation of God's laws, for our conscience will condemn us if we act wrongly. Hence, we need godly rulers and godly laws to be able to truly fulfill this requirement.

6. Citizens have a duty to render to civil government that which is due it.

We are to give to government what it is due. Jesus said we are to render to Caesar (the state) what is due him (Matt. 22:15-21; see Chapter 5). This includes paying taxes, which supports the government as it fulfills its biblical purpose. This purpose will be covered more thoroughly later, but in general, government is to punish evil-doers and protect law-abiding citizens' life, liberty, and property. In other words, it is to do "good" – to administer God's justice in its sphere of responsibility. If civil leaders do "bad," then we are under

obligation to take the appropriate steps to change corrupt government. We will discuss later what is due to government. While we are to submit to government, this is not an unlimited submission.

Jesus taught that we are to render to Caesar (civil government) what belongs to Caesar, but we are not to render to the Caesar what belongs to God.

Chapter 4

The Purpose and Responsibility of Civil Government

From the Scriptures examined above we have seen that God instituted civil government for the good of mankind. It serves an important function in advancing God's kingdom in the earth by way of protecting the righteous and punishing evil-doers. Its purpose can be more fully expressed by the "Five Ps."

The "Five Ps" of Government

In addition to the passage from Romans 13, First Peter 2:13-14 and First Timothy 2:1-2 provide insight into the biblical purpose of government. Peter writes:

> [13] Submit yourselves for the Lord's sake to every human institution, whether to a king as the one in authority, [14] or to governors as sent by him for the punishment of evildoers and the praise of those who do right. - 1 Peter 2:13-14 (NASB)

In this passage, Peter affirms submission to government as a divine institution to punish evil-doers and protect the innocent. In the book of Timothy, Paul writes:

> [1] First of all, then, I urge that entreaties and prayers, petitions and thanksgivings, be made on behalf of all men, [2] for kings and all who are in authority, so that we may lead a tranquil and quiet life in all godliness and dignity. - 1 Timothy 2:1-2 (NASB)

One purpose of praying for our leaders is that we may live a quiet, peaceful life.

From the passages in Romans, 1 Peter, and 1 Timothy we can summarize the purpose of government with five points. Civil government is to:

1. Protect the righteous
2. Punish evildoers
3. Promote biblical justice
4. Praise those who do right
5. Provide peace

Let's look at each point in more detail.

Civil government is a divine institution, intended by God to protect the righteous, punish criminals, and provide peace so that we might carry on the work of His kingdom.

1. Protect the Righteous (Law-abiding Citizens)

We saw previously that God created government to protect valuable life. Government is to also protect and secure all of man's God-given inalienable rights, which can be summarized by a right to life, liberty, and property. These rights are to be protected from domestic and foreign lawbreakers.

Firstly, government is to secure life. The sixth commandment, "you shall not murder" (Ex. 20:13), reveals we have a right to life. This right was established from the beginning. God created man in His image (Gen. 1:27) and breathed life into him (Gen. 2:7). Life is valuable because man (male and female) is created in God's image. God sent Joseph into Egypt to preserve life (Gen. 45:5, 7). Jesus came to bring life (John 10:10). God instituted government to execute justice against those who take innocent life (Gen. 9:6). Since our life is God-given and valuable, we have a right to self-defense and a right to government protection.

According to God's law, civil authorities have the power to quarantine those with contagious and dangerous diseases as a means to protect human life (Lev. 13:46; 14:33-53).

We also have a right to liberty. God's law declares, "He who kidnaps a man ...shall be put to death" (Ex. 21:16), making it a capital crime to take away one's liberty. In the Year of Jubilee all men were to be set free: "Proclaim liberty throughout the land unto all the inhabitants thereof" (Lev. 25:10). God desires men to live in liberty: "Where the Spirit of the Lord is, there is liberty" (2 Cor. 3:17). Jesus began His ministry by declaring that the Spirit of the Lord anointed him to set at liberty the oppressed (Luke 4:18).

Thomas Jefferson said that "our liberties are the gift of God."[33] The many freedoms secured by the United States Bill of Rights – freedom of worship, speech, assembly, press, petition – are rooted in man's biblical rights. Governments exist to secure these rights.

Man has a God-given right to property. This is implied by the Eighth and Tenth Commandments, "You shall not steal" (Ex. 20:15), and you shall not covet your neighbor's property (Ex. 20:17). The idea of private property rights is taught many places in the Scriptures (Deut. 19:14; Deut. 27:17; Jer. 32:1-16; Ex. 22:1 ff; Prov. 6:30-21; Matt. 20:1-16; Acts 5:4), as are the concepts of individual enterprise (man is entitled to the fruit of his labor) and free markets.[34] Assuring "just weights and measures" in the marketplace is one practical way the state can protect property according to the Bible (Deut. 25:13-14). Governments exist to protect our property rights, and property is not only external, but also internal (the principle of property will be examined more in Chapter 7).

One primary purpose of civil government is to protect the life, liberty, and property of men. In order to do this, a government should establish a police force to protect against domestic law-breakers and coordinate an army for defense against foreign enemies.

While performing this important function of protecting life, liberty, and property, civil rulers must also protect the people from government abuse. History has shown that while governments exist to protect the life, liberty, and property of its citizens, they have often plundered them. To keep this from happening, governments should be organized to check the sinful nature of man and his proclivity to abuse power. Such a structure would include decentralized government, separation of powers, election of representatives, and constitutionalism (see Chapter 9).

Protecting property and God-given rights is a fundamental purpose of government, but providing property and rights is not. We are to do what is good. Government protects us as we pursue our godly purposes and vocation to create needed goods and services that benefit mankind and advance God's kingdom in the earth. Government should not provide property, goods, or rights. Anything the government provides, it can take away. If we think our rights come from government, then government can easily take them away. If we think government should provide us material things, then government will control not only our property, but our entire life. Government is to protect us as we exercise our God-given rights and fulfill our mission to take dominion over the earth.

2. Punish Evildoers (Criminals)

God ordained government to punish evil-doers or criminals—those who break God's laws—such as murderers (Ex. 20:13; 21:12) and thieves (Ex. 20:15). The Bible has much to say about crime and punishment.

Crime is rooted in the sinful nature of man. Sin is acting contrary to God's standard as revealed in His Law-Word. Crime is unlawful behavior (as delineated by God in His Word) that usually threatens the life, liberty, or property of others, either directly (such as robbery or murder) or indirectly (such as treason). There is criminal activity that potentially only affects one's own person, such as dangerous drug use. Such activity is still an assault on life (and our lives are not our own since God who created us ultimately owns us; we are merely stewards of our bodies).

Crime comes under the jurisdiction of the state or civil government. While all crimes (as defined by God, but not necessarily the state) are sins, all sins are not crimes punishable by civil authorities. Many sins (violation of God's Law-Word) are outside the jurisdiction of the state. Some sins are to be dealt with by the family, some by the church, and many by God Himself. It is very important that civil leaders understand the distinction of crime and sin, the source of crime, and how to administer God's justice when crime is committed.

Civil governments throughout history have declared many actions to be criminal that according to God are not criminal at all, including reading the Bible and worshiping God according to the dictates of one's own conscience. Where laws exist that are contrary to God's higher law, it is the duty of Christians to seek to change these. Sometimes men have criminalized bad behavior, with the goal of limiting behavior that was not criminal according to God, but rather was sinful, or potentially sinful. The Eighteen Amendment to the United States Constitution is one such example. This well-intended but ill-conceived prohibition amendment, adopted in 1919, caused more problems than it attempted to solve and was eventually repealed in 1933.[35]

Some use the example of prohibition in America to proclaim we cannot legislate morality, nor should we try to legislate morality. However, every law is a legislation of someone's morality. Murder and theft are moral issues. Enacting laws against these actions is a legislation of morality. The important question is, "whose morality should we legislate?" There are really only two answers: either's God's morality (which He reveals in His Word, the Bible) or man's. While all law legislates morality, it is very important to understand that man cannot legislate goodness. Laws cannot change the heart of man; they cannot elevate men above the level of their faith and morality.

A society must understand the source of crime before they can effectively deal with crime. The Bible clearly states that wickedness and sin in the heart of man is the source of crime (Gen. 6:5, 11). As a result of man's original sin – that is, disobedience to God – evil entered his heart. What was in the heart of man manifested itself in his actions (the world was filled with violence). Recognizing the true nature of man – he is a sinful, fallen being in need of a savior – is the beginning place for a society to correctly deal with crime. Both preventative and corrective measures must be taken.[36]

To effectively accomplish the purpose of punishing criminals, governments should be structured following the biblical pattern, including having a constitution with just laws and penalties, and having impartial judges and fair trials.

3. Promote Biblical Justice

Civil leaders are ministers of God for good (Rom. 13:4). To administer good, leaders must administer God's law, which is good. They are to administer laws of biblical morality. They are not to legislate "good" (that is, attempt to make men good via law, which is impossible), but they should legislate biblical morality, as was mentioned above.

Government leaders are to judge for God in matters under their jurisdiction. The state's jurisdictional duties include areas of civil justice and national defense for the purpose of protecting the life, liberty, and property of the citizenry: (1) Enforcing the biblical laws of restitution for theft of property (Ex. 22:1-17); (2) Enforcing corporal punishment and/or fines for minor offenses [Lev. 19:14; Deut. 22:13-21; Num. 5:5-10; Lev. 5:14-16; Lev. 6:1-7. For sins of negligence and inadvertence (Num. 5:5-10; Lev. 5:14-16) and minor offenses of a deliberate nature involving property (Lev. 6:1-7), the principal plus 20% was to be restored.]; (3) Enforcing the biblical law of capital punishment for murder (Ex. 21:12-16; Num. 35:11-21); (4) Enforcing just weights and measures (Lev. 19:35-37; Deut. 25:13-16; Prov. 11:1; 16:11; 20:10, 23); (5) protecting the defenseless (Ps. 82:1-4).[37]

To promote biblical justice, leaders are to work to establish their nations upon the precepts in the Bible.[38] To have such leaders, Christians must seek by prayer and political effort to get men elected to office who understand godly justice and mercy. The Bible says we are to "seek justice, reprove the ruthless; defend the orphan, plead for the widow" (Isa. 1:17, 23). To do this we must be involved in places of power and influence, that is, in civil government. If oppressive taxes cause a widow's land to be taken from her, we must be in positions to stop this. If children are left impoverished because their father abandons them, then we must be in government to rectify this injustice.

We must not only pray for the oppressed but fight for them as well. Civil government has been and is the greatest oppressor in history. God's people must be involved in government to stop this oppression. We must be change agents in the public affairs of the nations.

Governors are to administer God's justice and righteousness. King David administered justice and judgment (2 Sam. 8:15), as did Solomon (1 Kings 10:9). God requires civil rulers and all men "to do justice" (Micah 6:8). He commands, "You shall do no injustice in judgment" (Lev. 19:15). He Himself administers justice for the fatherless and widow (Deut. 10:18). Civil leaders are to execute justice and righteousness (Ezek. 45:9-11; Deut. 33:21). Those who distort justice are cursed (Deut. 27:19).

How do we "do justice?" What is justice? God declares that, "All His ways are justice." He is "a God of truth and without injustice. Righteous and upright is He" (Deut. 32:4, NKJV). His ways revealed in His Word are the standard for justice. Acting justly is acting in accordance with what is right. In the Bible the Hebrew and Greek words translated *justice* mean *right, righteous, just, right conduct*. Thus, to do justice means to do right. God's Word reveals to man what is right and what is wrong. God's law is just, right, and good (Rom. 7:12). Thus, justice is adherence to His Word. Justice comes as His Word is applied in its entirety. Equal justice is only possible under God's law. It has not and cannot occur under man's law.

God's Word declares that there is right and there is wrong, thus there is a standard for absolute justice. There is no justice where relativism prevails because the standard of what is right and just is always changing; it is relative to the time, society, or circumstances. This is one reason why there is no equal justice for all under man's law.

Babylon under Hammurabi had law, but it did not have justice for all.[39] Egypt had law (which emanated from the Pharaohs), but enslaved many. Greece and Rome had law, but not justice for all (one third of the Roman Empire were slaves with no rights). Establishing a nation of laws is not sufficient to assure justice and liberty. The rule of law is an important concept; however, whose law you look to is of utmost importance. The source of law of a society is the god of that society. The law you obey emanates from your god. In Deuteronomy 28:14 Moses commanded the people to not turn aside from God's law, for in so doing they would be serving other gods. If we as individuals or a society follow laws other than God's, we are following other gods.

The source of law of a society will also determine how free, just, and prosperous the society will become. This is because ideas have consequences. Ideas are like seeds. The seeds you plant determine the fruit that is produced. Planting God's seeds produce a blessed and just society. History has shown that the most free, just, and prosperous nations have been those that have best applied God's Word in every sphere of life.

One aspect of the fruit of Christianity is right relationships — between God and man, as well as between people. These right relationships are foundational for just and transformed societies. Some people think we should use the vast power of civil government to establish justice and meet the great needs in society; however, government cannot change the heart of man, love people, build self-government, nor do other fundamental things necessary for transformation. Only the God of the Christian faith transforms the heart of man, bringing him into right relationship with the Creator God, and then establishes justice in man's heart and mind (justice grows in man as he learns and adheres to God's standards). This internal change of heart and growing sense of justice causes right relationships among people. Social justice is advanced as myriad acts of relational justice occur every day throughout the communities in a nation. The internal transformation of man also leads to right actions by individuals, families, churches, and civil governments — each fulfilling their biblical purpose and operating in their sphere of responsibility, and thus effecting godly justice and transformation. Hence, civil rulers are to promote God's justice in their sphere of authority.

What we see from the above three points is that civil government, in general, is to uphold the rule of law. It is to protect those who abide by the law, punish those who violate the law, and administer God's law as it relates to its limited civil responsibilities.

4. Praise Those Who Do Right

God intends governors to praise those who do right (1 Peter 2:13-14). Doing so encourages lawful behavior. In contrast, praising those who do wrong will encourage unlawful behavior. Our words impact us and others. "Death and life are in the power of the tongue" (Prov. 18:21). Since the words of leaders reach a wide audience, they have a great impact for good or evil. "A fool's lips bring strife....A fool's mouth is his ruin" (Prov. 18:6-7), while "the tongue of the wise brings healing" (Prov. 12:18), and "a good word makes [the heart] glad" (Prov. 12:25).

Leaders are to uphold the righteous as examples, for as they do, they are showing the citizens the character and worldview necessary for the nation to be free. The more that citizens exemplify godly character and thought, the more the nation at large will act justly, prosper, advance in all areas, and experience the liberty that Christ came to give to mankind.

5. Provide Peace

God wants us to live a quiet and tranquil (peaceful) life (1 Tim. 2:1-2). For this to occur, governing officials must be just and rule in the fear of the Lord. Thus, Paul instructs us to pray for kings and those in authority with this end in mind. This prayer for leaders is for them to act in such a lawful way as to provide a stable society where there is peace and safety.

A peaceable life for the citizenry is to be a goal of civil leaders. God wants people to be able to live a godly life, so leaders should encourage this and not make it hard by enacting suppressive laws or forcing ungodly action upon the people.

To establish peace in a nation, that nation must honor the Prince of Peace. It must seek to establish the Kingdom of God; that is, His righteousness, peace, and joy (Rom. 14:17).[40] We should work to place men in office who will encourage a peaceful environment in the nation, and hence enable each of us to live in accordance with God's desire. To be effective, government leaders must understand the nature of evil and the biblical purpose of government. They should execute justice in a swift manner (Eccl. 8:11) and punish criminals in accordance with biblical penalties.[41] Doing so will help create an atmosphere of peace and lawfulness.

Chapter 5

Jesus' Teachings on Civil Government

Many people do not think of Jesus as having taught anything about government, but He did. In fact, His teachings on government have transformed, and are still transforming, the world. Some of His teachings follow.

1. God created and is sovereign over civil government. Civil government is a divinely ordained institution.

Jesus declared that "all authority has been given to Me in heaven and on earth" (Matt. 28:18). There is no authority outside of Him. His authority is over all. Likewise, He owns all. God created everything and so everything belongs to Him and is under His domain. The earth is the Lord's and all it contains (Gen. 1-2; Ex. 9:29; 19:5; Dt. 10:14; Lev. 25:23; 1 Chron. 29:11; Job 41:11; Ps. 24:1; 50:10-12; 1 Cor. 10:26). Jesus affirms that all of man's authority is delegated authority.

When Jesus answered Pilate, "You would have no authority over Me, unless it had been given you from above" (John. 19:11), He asserts that civil authority is delegated and controlled by God. Paul states this in Romans 13:1 by saying, "there is no authority except from God, and those which exist are established by God." This also means that God is sovereign in human history and government; He is "the ruler over the kings of the earth" (Rev 1:5). This idea is important because many Christians today tend to view civil government as something "worldly" and unspiritual and, therefore, it is not necessary for the believer to study or be involved in government. Spirituality involves more than religious and ecclesiastical topics.

Civil government, like the family and church, is a covenantal institution. It operates under God's authority and is to administer His justice/law. His law is the covenant that God requires leaders to uphold. The Founders of America covenanted under God to establish governments. For example, the Mayflower compact states: "We...solemnly and mutually, in the Presence of God and one another, covenant and combine ourselves together into a civil Body Politick."[42] The covenantal nature of American government sets it apart from almost all governments in history and is an important reason for the great liberty and prosperity of the United States of America.

2. Sovereign jurisdictions and separation of institutions. Limited government.

In attempting to trap Jesus, the Pharisees sent their disciples to ask Him whether it was lawful to pay taxes to Caesar or not (see Matthew 22:15-21; Mark 12:14-17). Knowing their malice, Jesus responded by having them show a coin and asking them whose image was inscribed upon it. When they replied, "Caesar's," he said, "Then render to Caesar the things that are Caesar's; and to God the things that are God's." Jesus was teaching an extremely important concept here — that of jurisdictional authority. Jesus used a coin with Caesar's image upon it to illustrate that civil government does indeed have certain jurisdictional authority, such as in the area of taxation. However, Christ went on to pronounce that the state's jurisdiction is limited when He said that we are to render "to God the things that are God's." The inference is that there is a sphere of life where civil government (i.e. Caesar) has no jurisdiction at all. That sphere is implied here as involving the soul and mind of men, being made, not in Caesar's image, but in the image of God. Jesus was affirming that religious worship and

Caesar thought his authority extended to all spheres of life, but Jesus declared it was limited.

opinions, and any endeavor relating to thought or speech, must remain completely free from government control.

This is the biblical idea of the separation of church and state. It is not like the modern idea, which says we must remove God from public life. The principle of separation of church and state, the separation of school and state, and the separation of the press and speech from the control of the state, which are articulated in the First Amendment of the United States Constitution, are rooted in this historic political teaching of Christ. Before Christianity, the pagan world always included religion and education under the jurisdiction of the state. It was a radical political concept for Christ to declare that Caesar's power should be limited and, therefore, was used against Jesus when He was convicted of treason and crucified under Roman law. Christ's teaching has since changed the western world.

Caesar thought he was Lord, but Christians declared that "Jesus is Lord." Caesar saw this declaration by early believers as a threat to the state and to his reign and, hence, persecuted and killed many Christians.

The responsibilities of the state are to be distinguished from that of the individual, family, and church. Usurpation of authority occurs when one jurisdiction encroaches upon another jurisdiction. The result is tyranny. Usurpation is exercising authority or power that belongs to another. It is "the act of seizing or occupying and enjoying the property of another, without right."

Commenting on this passage of Scripture, Lord Acton wrote: "When Christ said 'Render unto Caesar the things that are Caesar's and unto God the things that are God's,' He gave to the state a legitimacy it had never before enjoyed, and set bounds to it that had never yet been acknowledged. And He not only delivered the precept but he also forged the instrument to execute it. To limit the power of the State ceased to be the hope of patient, ineffectual philosophers and became the perpetual charge of a universal Church."[43]

Part of the mission of the church is to advance the crown rights of King Jesus over His creation. To do so requires the church to limit the power of civil government, which historically has usually sought to govern God's earth according to the selfish designs of corrupt rulers rather than in accordance with God's Law.

Limited Government / Jurisdictional Boundaries

While God cannot be separated from government, since He ordained it, Jesus does speak of limits of jurisdiction of the state. The jurisdiction of the family and the church are also limited and defined in the Bible. Jesus taught that we are to render "to Caesar [the state] the things that are Caesar's, and to God the things that are God's." Government does have certain legitimate rights to which we should give our allegiance, but they are very limited. One thing that belongs to the state and not the individual or any other institution is the use of the sword to protect the citizenry (Rom. 13:1-4). This means that we are to serve in the military if asked to do so (1 Sam 8:11-17). (God did allow nonparticipation by those whose conscience was violated. Additionally, we are not obligated to take up arms to support obviously non-biblical activities.)

Understanding the limited role of government in our lives and working to hold our government leaders accountable to their limited functions are important because history shows that government leaders readily promise to give people many things, but end up taking much from them. The nation of Israel learned this when they asked for a king in First Samuel 8. God via Samuel warned them that the centralized power would end up robbing from them.

God brought harsh judgment on those civil and religious leaders in Israel who stepped outside their jurisdictional boundaries. For example, when King Uzziah attempted to perform ecclesiastical functions contrary to God's law, he was struck with leprosy, cut off from the Temple, isolated from the people, and lost his kingdom to his son (2 Chron. 26:16-21). Azariah the priest, along with eighty other priests of the Lord, resisted this civil ruler's attempt to usurp the authority of the religious leaders (v. 17-18), providing a good example of what leaders in the church should do today if the state attempts to encroach upon the church's duties and responsibilities.

Another legitimate function of the state that Jesus clearly affirms in Matthew 22 is the collection of taxes (see also Matt. 17:24-27; Rom. 13:6-8). "Rendering to Caesar" (government) in a representative republic would also mean that we are to serve on juries, be involved in the political parties, and vote. Some things that belong to God and not the state include our worship of God (religion), our children and their education (schools), our property (free market), and our ideas (free speech and press). In these matters, the state has no authority and should not interfere or attempt to control. The church, the market, the press, and the schools are to remain completely free and independent.

3. The supreme value of all persons and their superiority over the state

When Jesus referred to the image of Caesar on the money in Matthew 22, He, by implication and contrast, said that anything having the image of God on it is not under Caesar's jurisdiction. We are stamped with the image of God since we were created by Him. The value of individual life is taught throughout scripture.

The sanctity of human life was the foundation for the establishment of government beginning with Noah (Gen 9:6). Because man is made in the image of God, Jesus taught that each person has worth regardless of what they can do. This contradicted the pagan idea that an individual was regarded as valuable only if he could contribute something to the state, or if he belonged to a certain social class or race. The individual is superior to the state or any collective interest. This is the principle of individuality. Clearly, Jesus and the early Christians exhibited the value that God places on all human beings regardless of race, class, handicap or gender (John 3:16; Matt. 10:30-31).

4. Citizens are to contribute, support, and submit to limited government.

Jesus and the Bible teach that men have duties toward civil government (Mark 12:14-17; Rom. 13:7). Paul wrote to Titus: "remind them to be subject to rulers, to authorities, to be obedient" (Tit. 3:1). For civil leaders to perform their biblical duties, the people must unite with them and perform their duties as good citizens. Both the rulers and the ruled have a part to play in building a peaceful, free, and prosperous society.

Our leaders govern with our consent. After we select our leaders, we must stand with them by gladly obeying the laws, paying lawful taxes, and helping to defend the nation when necessary. We should also encourage our rulers in their duties and humbly petition them when they act contrarily. We are to treat them respectfully, even if we disagree with their actions. If they act in an evil manner, we should work to replace them via legal means.

5. Government leaders are to be public servants.

In response to some of His disciples arguing over "which one of them was regarded to be greatest," Jesus said:

> "The kings of the Gentiles exercise lordship over them, and those who exercise authority over them are called 'benefactors.' But not so among you; on the contrary, he who is greatest among you, let him be as the younger, and he who governs as he who serves" (NKJV) (Luke 22:24-26; see also Matt. 20:25-26).

Jesus is making reference to civil authorities—"kings of the Gentiles"—and is declaring that they are to be public servants. The purpose of civil government is to serve people.

That civil officials are to be servants of the people was a radical new idea. It contrasted greatly with the pagan idea of rulers dominating the people, an idea which existed throughout the entire world at this time. This declaration of Caesar not being the lord over the people was later to become evidence for charges of treason brought against Christ. This idea gradually spread

Jesus taught the revolutionary concept that civil leaders are to be public servants.

and impacted many nations, especially the United States. Today, America calls her civil leaders "public servants." Many nations call their civil officials "ministers" (the word *minister* means *servant*) and their main leader the "Prime Minister," or in other words their "chief servant!" This world-changing concept originated with Jesus Christ who, according to many Christians, had nothing to say about government. That the civil government is the servant of man is a Christian idea.

Not only is government to serve man, but it is to serve all men equally. All men are created equally in the image of God. This does not mean that all men are born with the same physical abilities or talents, or the same intelligence or property. These are external things which vary. But all men (and women) are born with the same internal rights: the right to live, worship, speak, think, work, and travel according to how he sees fit. Marxism and socialism try to guarantee every man the equality of externals, but God's word simply states that every individual regardless of race, class, gender, or handicap should be protected by government in his opportunity to exercise his internal rights. Jesus and the early church condemned discrimination and prejudice and partiality in treatment (James 2; 3:9; Acts 15:2-11; Gal. 3:28).

6. Gradual change from the internal to the external

God's pathway to liberty is from the internal to the external. While God desires us to work to establish an external expression of His Kingdom on earth (Matt 6:10 — "Your Kingdom come, Your will be done on earth as it is in heaven"), this kingdom must first begin in the heart of man, and then it will naturally express itself externally in all aspects of society. The Bible reveals that "where the Spirit of the Lord is, there is liberty" (2 Corinthians 3:17). As was stated previously, when the Spirit of the Lord comes into the heart of a man, that man is liberated. Likewise, when the Spirit of the Lord comes into a nation, that nation is liberated. The degree to which the Spirit of the Lord is infused into a society (through its people, laws, and institutions), is the degree to which that society will experience liberty in every realm (civil, religious, economic, etc.). Christ came to set us free (Gal. 5:1, 3). Spiritual freedom or liberty ultimately produces political freedom.

Matthew 12:18-21 states that Jesus came to "declare justice to the Gentiles" and "establish justice in the earth" (Isa 42:1-4), and that He does it in a gentle manner. "He will not quarrel nor cry out, nor will anyone hear His voice in the streets" as He helps overcome evil with good. Although Jesus intends to "liberate the oppressed" and to help those in slavery and poverty (Luke 4:17-18), His basic method of change is the same for nations as it is for individuals — we are gradually transformed as we apply the truth of His word to our lives. Dr. Augustus Neander reveals in his book, *General History of the Christian Religion* (1871), how Christianity has historically brought about change in various nations of the world:

Again, Christianity, from its nature, must pronounce sentence of condemnation against all ungodliness, but at the same time appropriate to itself all purely human relations and arrangements, consecrating and ennobling, instead of annihilating them....That religion which aimed nowhere to produce violent and convulsive changes from without, but led to reforms by beginning in the first place within, — whose peculiar character it was to operate positively rather than negatively, — to displace and destroy no faster than it substituted something better.[44]

Christian reforms within a nation do not begin with external or violent means, rather they begin internally in the heart and mind of man.

In dealing with unbiblical situations in the nations today, we must remember that reform begins within, and as we remove that which is culturally detrimental we must simultaneously substitute something positive. A government-controlled and funded welfare system is unbiblical, yet the solution is not to pass a law that immediately eliminates civil government support of the needy. Individuals and churches must begin to fulfill their God-given responsibility in this area (substitute the good) as we work to remove the role of the civil government.

Neander goes on to say:

Yet Christianity nowhere began with outward revolutions and changes, which, in all cases where they have not been prepared from within, and are not based upon conviction, fail of their salutary ends. The new creation to which Christianity gave birth, was in all respects an inward one, from which the outward effects gradually and therefore more surely and healthfully, unfolded themselves to their full extent.[45]

External liberty, then, must come gradually, not immediately. Gradual transformation is one principle that can be gleaned from Jesus' parable of the talents or minas in Luke 19:11-17. The "nobleman" in the parable, who is a type of Christ, emphasizes to his servants that their responsibility is to "occupy" or "do business" with their earthly finances, time, and talents until He returns. The reward for the faithful was that they would be given "authority over cities."

Through this parable, Jesus was teaching Christians, among other things, how to implement godly transformation in society. It is not by gaining political power and externally imposing biblical law upon people, but by consistent hard work and service to meet the needs of society around us. As we do so, we convince even non-Christians of the validity and excellence of biblical ideas and solutions. Transformation comes about through the democratic process (i.e., power flowing from the people to rulers), not by coercion (where power originates from the rulers and flows down to the people). Legislation that is in conformity to biblical law is possible only to the extent that Christians get involved in shaping the culture and "occupying" until He comes.

Through Christ, God releases the "Law of Liberty" into society through the cleansed hearts of men (James 1:25; 2:12). This does not mean that the Old Testament law is done away with, but that man can now carry out the law, for God has empowered us to do so. The more a nation applies His law, the more that nation will prosper and walk in liberty. The degree to which a people apply His law personally will be reflected through their governmental institutions, for the law flows from the heart of man out to the nation. The church disciples nations (Matt 28:19) by teaching and training people to effect change through gradual democratic means; that is, from the bottom up, not the top down — from the internal to the external.

7. Uphold the civil laws of Moses and fundamental rights

Jesus clearly affirmed that the Laws of Moses were to be maintained in the culture unless specifically modified by the New Testament (Matt 5:17-19). He did not abolish any of the moral laws; only the ceremonial laws that were fulfilled by His sacrifice for sin were rendered obsolete.[46] Jesus affirmed the laws against murder, adultery, dishonoring of parents, theft, and perjury (Matt 5:21, 27; 19:18-19; Matt. 15:4). He also affirmed the laws concerning divorce (Matt 5:31; 19:7-9), oaths (Matt 5:33), and equitable punishment and restitution (Matt 5:38). Jesus clearly affirmed the right to private property, a free market for exchange, and making a profit when accompanied by compassionate use of wealth for the poor and needy (Matt. 25:14-30; Luke 19:11-27; 16:11; this is "Christian capitalism."). Jesus, in fact, affirmed all of the Ten Commandments in general (see Mark 10:17-19; Luke 18:18-20; Luke 10:25-28) as well as each of the Ten Commandments individually.[47] He taught:

- Seek first God's Kingdom (Mt. 6:33) (Commandments 1-3)
- Love the Lord (Mt. 22:37) (Commandments 1-3)
- Keep His commandments (John 14:15) (Commandments 1-3)
- Render to God what belongs to God (Mt. 22:19-21) (First Commandment)

- Render to Caesar only what belongs to Caesar (Mt. 22:19-21) (Second Commandment)
- Jesus affirmed that we are to do good and the work of God on the Sabbath (John 7:22-23; John 6:1-10; Luke 14:1-6) (Fourth Commandment).[48]
- Love your neighbor (Mt. 22:39) (Commandments 5-10)
- Honor your parents (Mt. 15:4) (Fifth Commandment)
- Do not murder, even in your thoughts (Matt. 5:21-22) (Sixth Commandment)
- Do not commit adultery, even in your thoughts (Matt. 5:27-28); honor marriage (Matt. 19:6); He told the woman caught in adultery to go and sin no more (John 8:11). (Seventh Commandment)
- Jesus affirmed restitution should be made for theft as demanded by the law. (Luke 19:8-10) (Eighth Commandment)
- Keep your word (Mt. 5:37) (Ninth Commandment)
- Beware of covetousness (Luke 12:15); deny yourself (Luke 9:23) (Tenth Commandment)

In upholding the Ten Commandments, Jesus was also teaching God-given inalienable rights since each commandment affirms the right or sanctity of something. Principles or rights contained in the Ten Commandments include:

1. Fear, love, and obey God; His Law-Word is supreme; sovereignty of God; freedom of worship; limited authority of man (government)
2. Duty to worship (in Spirit)
3. Freedom of speech, vows, oaths
4. Work and biblical rest (sanctity of time); Dominion Mandate
5. Biblical family; honor parents; respect authority
6. Life; value of the individual
7. Love (contract, oath); biblical marriage and morality
8. Private property
9. Truth (reputation)
10. Conscience; internal transformation and obedience; contentment.

Jesus did not rescind the death penalty with the woman caught in adultery (John 8:1-7; under the Law of Moses the death penalty was not mandatory for such an offense; lesser penalties were optional[49]). Jesus' actions assured that the legal process was followed properly using impartial juries and at least two witnesses in order to prove guilt[50] — thus upholding the principle of due process and the right of appeal in the Law of Moses (John 8:7; Deut. 17:4-7; 19:15; Matt 18:16). This formed the basis of our modern legal system that protects those charged with crimes until proven guilty by a fair trial. While it is biblical to use the legal system to uphold civil rights, Jesus taught that one should avoid litigation as much as possible (Luke 12:58).

8. Using political means to achieve social justice

Jesus taught that there is a time when one should get involved in the legal and political system in order to defend one's rights and to address injustice. The parable of the widow's case (Luke 18:2-5) is primarily about persistence in prayer, yet it is based on a civil setting for achieving justice which Christ clearly affirms (Lk. 18:6-8). It is not unbiblical to pursue social change through governmental systems.

Social injustice is the outcome of government rulers rejecting God's principles of government and acting in a tyrannical manner. If this occurs we have a duty to act in a biblical manner to correct the injustice.

9. Duty to resist and protest tyrannical government

As has been stated previously, the Bible clearly teaches that if any authority demands of us obedience contrary to God's Word, we must obey God rather than man (Ex. 1:15-21; Dan. 3:16-18; 6:6-10; Acts 4:19-20; 5:29). In his 1776 Election Sermon, Rev. Samuel West said, "Unlimited submission and obedience is due to none but God alone."[51]

Once we establish the need to resist, we must then determine the biblical means of resistance. Biblical heroes of the faith teach us that we should not be afraid when we disobey evil rulers and laws. Moses' parents disobeyed Pharaoh's command because "they were not afraid of the king's edict" (Heb. 11:23). Moses, "not fearing the wrath of the king," turned his back on Egypt and followed the Lord. A mark of the heroes of faith was disobedience to tyrannical rulers (see Hebrews 11). Jesus and the Bible give us three steps we are to take when resisting evil rulers.

Christ's Guidelines for Addressing Injustice

1. Protest or Legal Action

The first step to correct injustice is to protest and/or to take all legal action possible. Jesus instructed His disciples to publicly protest if city officials denied them their inalienable right to religious speech. He told them to go out into the streets and say, "Even the dust of your city which clings to our feet, we wipe off in protest against you" (Luke 10:10-11). "Wiping off the dust" is equivalent to boycotting. The free nations of the world generally have more means of legal recourse and of protesting ungodly action than do others. Examples of protesting include picketing abortion chambers, boycotting stores that sell pornography, and removing our children from public schools that deny God. We who live in free nations not only have the right to do this but are obligated to God to do so to keep our consciences clean.

Protesting unlawful action is a Christian idea. "Protestants" originally received this title due to their protesting against activities and authorities (civil and ecclesiastical) which were ungodly. In Acts 16 we read how Paul and Silas were unlawfully thrown into jail. When the chief magistrates tried to cover this up, Paul, recognizing his civil liberties were a sacred cause, demanded restitution to be made. Paul said to them, "They have beaten us in public without trial, men who are Romans, and have thrown us into prison; and now are they sending us away secretly? No indeed! But let them come themselves and bring us out" (Acts 16:37). The chief magistrates did come and bring them out themselves. Biblical methods of resistance work for non-Christians as well, with Gandhi of India being a prime example.

Biblical ways to protest include:

(1). Private appeals (1 Sam. 19:1-5; Esther 3:11-14; 4:13-16; 7:5-6, 10; 1 Kg. 12:1-15)

(2). Non-cooperation, boycotting

Jesus protested when He remained silent before Pilate and refused to cooperate (Mt 27:14). When Paul and Barnabas were driven out of Antioch by the city officials, "they shook off the dust of their feet in protest against them" (Acts 13:51) as Jesus had instructed them (Lk. 10:10-11).

(3). Litigation (Luke 12:58; 18:1-5; Acts 21-26)

The reason Paul appealed to Caesar within the Roman court system in Acts 24-26 was because his civil rights as a Roman citizen had been violated. He was being a good steward of the civil liberties God had given to him. The whole course of Paul's life was changed due to his exerting his rights as a citizen. He saw this action as part of the Great Commission. He considered his civil liberties a sacred cause.

(4). Public visible rallies, marches, demonstrations (Luke 10:10, 11; Isa. 20, Jer. 13; Ezek. 3, 4, 24, 33; 1 Kg. 18:19-21; Matt. 3:1-4)

Jesus publicly censured Herod for his death threats (Luke 13:31-32).

(5). Blocking access; non-violent intervention (Mark 11:15, 16)

(6). Disobeying unjust laws (Acts 5:29; 4:19-20; Dan 6:10; 2:49; 3:4-5, 16-18; Ex. 1:15-17; 2:2-3; Esther 4:10-16; 3:1-4, 6-11; Ezra 4:17, 21-24; 5:1-3; Haggai 2:1-2, 4-9; 1:12-14).

2. Flight/emigration

If all avenues of protest and legal action are expended in attempting to correct unlawful acts of civil authorities, then flight, if possible, is the next appropriate measure to take. Jesus told His disciples that "whenever they persecute you in this city, flee to the next" (Mt. 10:17, 18, 23). He also warned them to flee the destruction that was to come upon Jerusalem (Mt. 24:15-18). Seeking a safe refuge/sanctuary for hiding can be considered a form of flight. The early church took flight as persecution rose against them (Acts 8:1-4).

Sometimes flight to other places will more surely allow us to fulfill God's will. Joseph fled to Egypt to protect Jesus from Herod. The disciples fled Jerusalem (Acts 8). Many people who came to settle in America were fleeing civil and religious tyranny. After exhausting all means of protest and legal action, they saw that flight was the best means of accomplishing God's purpose. This principle is the basis of the Constitutional right of emigration. Tyrannical governments often restrict emigration.[52]

3. Force in self-defense

As a last recourse in resisting tyranny, use of force is a legitimate biblical means. The Old Testament contains many examples of God's people using force to defend themselves. The Bible teaches that a defensive war in a just cause is sinless.[53] Jesus affirmed it is okay to use force at certain times in resisting tyranny.

At the conclusion of the Last Supper, Jesus continued the instruction to his disciples that He had begun earlier (Luke 10) by telling them to arm themselves militarily:

> "Let him who has no sword sell his robe and buy one." And they said, "Lord, look, here are two swords." And He said to them, "It is enough." (Luke 22:36-50; see also Matthew 26:50-56).

Here, Jesus confirms the legitimacy of using force at certain times.

John Jay, the first Supreme Court Justice of the United States and one of the authors of the *Federalist Papers*, commented on this incident in a letter written in 1818:

> Although just war is not forbidden by the gospel in express terms, yet you think an implied prohibition of all war, without exception, is deducible from the answer of our Lord to Pilate, viz: "If my kingdom were of this world, then would my servants fight, etc."
>
> At the conclusion of the Last Supper, our Lord said to his disciples: "He that hath no sword, let him now sell his garment and buy one." They answered: "Lord, here are two swords." He replied: "It is enough."
>
> It is not to be presumed that our Lord would have ordered swords to be provided, but for some purpose for which a sword was requisite...
>
> When the officers and their band arrived, with swords and with staves, to take Jesus, they who were about him saw what would follow. "They said unto him: Lord, shall we smite with the sword?" [Luke 22:49]. It does not appear that any of the eleven disciples who were with him, except one, made the least attempt to defend him. But, Peter, probably inferring from the other swords, that they were now to be used, proceeded to "smite a servant of the high-priest, and cut off his right ear" [vs. 50]. Jesus (perhaps, among other reasons, to abate inducements to prosecute Peter for that violent attack) healed the ear.
>
> He ordered Peter to put his sword into its sheath, and gave two reasons for it. The first related to himself, and amounted to this, that he would make no opposition, saying: "The cup which my Father hath given me, shall I not drink?" The second related to Peter, viz., they who take the sword, shall perish by the sword [Matt 26:52]; doubtless meaning that they who take and use a sword, as Peter had just done, without lawful authority, and against lawful authority, incur the penalty and risk of perishing by the sword. This meaning seems to be attached to those words by the occasion and circumstances which prompted

them. If understood in their unlimited latitude, they would contradict the experience and testimony of all ages, it being manifest that many military men die peaceably in their beds.[54]

As Jay noted, Christ's mission precluded the use of force in this particular instance, nonetheless, Jesus taught the legitimacy of using the legal sword to restrain the illegal sword of an aggressor. Peter here however, in his impatience became the aggressor rather than remaining in the posture of self-defense.

The Bible states that the authority and responsibility of using the sword to punish evil or protect the righteous (either from law-breakers within a nation or from an aggressive outside enemy) resides with the civil government (Rom. 13:1-4). (This does not negate the Scriptural right to use force to protect ourselves and our families from personal harm.) That is why anytime we reach the step where force is necessary in resisting tyranny, we must go through legitimate governing officials. A lower representative must be convinced to ignore a higher decree and declare that a higher ruler is acting in rebellion to God's higher law. This theory of interposition is based in Scripture and was affirmed by Manegold of Lautenbach in 1080 and again in the Protestant Reformation of Europe. One of the best treatises on it was written by the French Protestants in 1579 entitled *A Defense of Liberty Against Tyrants*.

In the American Christian Revolution, the colonists were not in rebellion (from God's perspective) in their struggle for independence from Britain, but were acting in accordance with the biblical guidelines for resisting tyranny. They followed the above three steps in order. If we do not follow these steps in order, we will bring undue harm to ourselves, to others, and to God's cause. But those who do follow God's guidelines properly and disobey an ungodly law or ruler must be prepared to pay the price for such an action, recognizing permanent change will come gradually as more people are changed from within. Some may have to suffer while this is taking place.

Thus, we see that Jesus Christ, the focal point of all human history, is also the turning point in the history of liberty. He provided the basis for internal liberty with His sacrificial death for sin. But He also provided an extensive set of teachings on external liberty which was part of what He wanted taught among the nations when He gave His disciples the Great Commission: "Go therefore and make disciples of all the nations ... teaching them to observe all things that I have commanded you." (Mt 28:19-20).

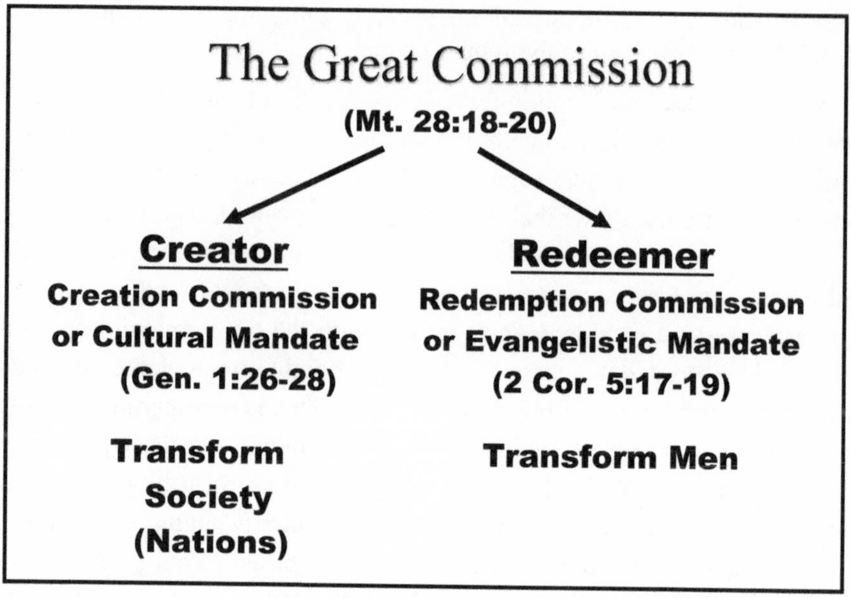

The Great Commission
(Mt. 28:18-20)

Creator
**Creation Commission
or Cultural Mandate
(Gen. 1:26-28)**

**Transform
Society
(Nations)**

Redeemer
**Redemption Commission
or Evangelistic Mandate
(2 Cor. 5:17-19)**

Transform Men

The Great Commission includes both the mandate to transform men and to transform society.

Chapter 6

The Relationship between God and Government

Biblical Conception of Society

To properly understand the role of civil government in society we must understand how God structured society at large. The following diagram represents the biblical conception of society.

God created individuals and three divine institutions through which mankind carries out his mission in the earth. There are other spheres of life where

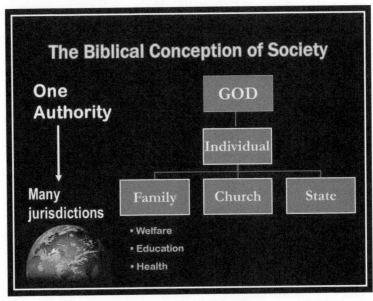

authority is exercised (see Chapter 1), but there are only three divine institutions, each characterized by its own form of government taught in the

Scriptures. (The biblical forms of government for the family, church, and state are constructed so as to check the tendency of sinful man to abuse power.) The other spheres (like school, work, and associations) are extensions of the authority of one of the divine institutions (primarily the family and individuals). To most effectively accomplish man's biblical mission, we must understand to whom God has given authority to do what.

The Purpose and Responsibilities of the Four Basic Spheres of Government

The following outline briefly summarizes the purpose and responsibilities of individuals and the divine institutions.

Individual

Purpose and Responsibilities:
1. Worship – "Love the Lord your God." (Luke 10:27, Deut. 6:5)
    * Man's primary purpose is to glorify God and enjoy him forever
    a. Personal prayer, Bible reading/study/meditation
    b. Assemble with other believers
    c. Christian Sabbath observance
2. Charity – "Love your neighbor." (Luke 10:27, Lev. 19:9-18, Mt. 25:35-36)
    * The Golden rule: Do unto others as you would have them do unto you
    a. Assist the needy and show mercy
    b. Speak the truth – evangelism, exhortation, edification
    c. Involvement in society/government (conversion of institutions)
3. Work – "as [you love] yourself" (Lk. 10:27; Gen. 1:26-28, Gen. 2:15)
    * That man is God's creation and made in God's image is the foundation for self-worth, self-preservation, human dignity, and work. Our calling or work is the means of fulfilling the cultural mandate of being fruitful and subduing the earth.
    a. Provide for self and family – individuals will start businesses and create wealth
    b. Bless the nations – occurs as individuals provide needed goods and services

Family

A family is simply a man, woman, and children who are related by marriage, blood, or adoption. The ideal marriage has a man and woman who covenant together to fulfill God's desire for them to be fruitful and bless the world. Both parents are to fulfill the purpose and responsibilities. In this context fathers (in general, but not exclusively) lead in society, while mothers raise the next generations (Gen. 1:18, 22-24; 3:16).

Purpose and Responsibilities:

1. Dominion and procreation (Gen. 1:28, 1 Tim. 5:10, 14)
   * Be fruitful and multiply, subdue the earth
   a. Pro-life – sanctity of life (Gen. 9:6)
   b. Children – a blessing (Ps. 127:3-5)
2. Education (Dt. 6:6-7)
   * "You shall teach your sons."
   a. Fit children to fulfill their individual purposes and responsibilities (Pr. 22:6)
   b. Build godly character (Gen. 18:19)
   c. Train in a biblical worldview (Ps. 78:5)
   d. Discipline as well as instruction (Eph. 6:4)
3. Health and welfare
   * Practice hospitality (Rom. 12:13), especially for those of your own household.
   a. Preventative health care – proper exercise, nutrition, sanitation
   b. Taking care of the sick, elderly, orphan, widow (1 Tim. 5:4, 8, 10, 16; Dt. 15:7, 8, 11; Dt. 14:28-29)
   c. Saving and investing for your retirement and your posterity (2 Cor. 12:14, Pr. 19:14, Dt. 21:17)

Church

Purpose and Responsibilities:

   * The church prepares people to govern society (to rule, Ps. 8:6) and to fulfill the redemption and creation commissions.
1. Regular instruction of members in biblical truth for every sphere of life

   a. Sunday preaching, regular classes, and other educational means (Mt. 28:18-20, 2 Tim. 3:16-17)

   b. Includes starting schools and colleges

2. Administer sacraments and church discipline (1 Cor. 5:8-13; 11:23-25; Mt. 18:15-17)

   a. Corporate worship and sacrifice (Gen. 4:3-5, 26)

   b. Baptism and Lord's Supper (communion)

   c. Excommunication

3. Discipling, equipping, and organizing believers (Eph. 4:11-12, 16; Titus 3:8, 14)

   a. Equipping the saints for the work of service, enabling them to fulfill their divine occupation or calling.

   b. Providing coordination and support for individuals and families to work in voluntary union with others to fulfill their purpose.

   c. Pastors are to be role models of what the church teaches in their personal conduct and through their involvement in society.

Civil Government (State)

Purpose and Responsibilities:[55]

1. Protect the righteous, i.e. law-abiding citizens (Rom. 13:3-4, 1 Pet. 2:13-14)

   a. Protection of life, liberty, and property from domestic and foreign lawbreakers. Governments are to secure God-given inalienable rights:

Life	Liberty	Property
Ex. 20:13 – "You shall not murder"	Ex. 21:16 – "He who kidnaps a man...shall be put to death."	Ex. 20:15 – "You shall not steal."
Self-defense Gov't protection	Free worship Free speech Free assembly Free press Free schools Right to petition government	Private property Individual enterprise Acquire necessities of life

   b. Government coordinates civilian police for order and army for defense.

   c. Protection of rights from government abuse as well, via:

      • Decentralized government

      • Separation of powers

      • Election of representatives

2. Punish the evil doer, i.e. criminal (Ex. 20:13; 21:12; 22:2)

a. Set up constitution with just laws and penalties

b. Impartial judges and fair trial to establish justice

3. Administer God's justice

a. Civil leaders are ministers of God for good (Rom. 13:4).

b. They are to judge for God in matters under their jurisdiction.

God gives the means to each institution to enforce its authority.

In each of these spheres, the biblical flow of authority is to be from the internal to the external. As God's Word and Spirit are established in individuals, there will be proper functioning of the family, church, and state. However, since man is fallen, his tendency is to act unlawfully. When this occurs, God has given each divine institution a means to enforce its authority:

1) Family — rod (Pr. 13:24; Pr. 22:15; Pr. 23:13-14; Pr. 29:15, 17; Heb. 12:7)

2) Church — excommunication (Mt. 18:15-18; 1 Tim 1:20; Tit. 3:10; 1 Cor. 5:11)

3) State — sword (Rom. 13:4; Gen. 9:6)

Civil Penalties for Criminal Offenses

If God's law-word is violated, it should be handled by the appropriate jurisdiction and with an appropriate penalty. We should discern (which requires a thorough knowledge of the Bible) if it is the responsibility of the family, church, or state to administer God's justice. In reality, the Bible teaches that God will Himself execute His justice when many of His laws are violated, hence limiting the punitive action of man (and the potential of abuse). The general penalties for violating God's civil laws include:

1) Restitution for theft (Ex. 22:1 ff). Work (via servitude) to make restitution for those unable to pay.

2) Corporal punishment and/or fines for minor offenses (Lev. 19:14; Deut. 22:13-21; Num. 5:5-10; Lev. 5:14-16; Lev. 6:1-7)

3) Death for serious offenses against life or incorrigibility[56] (Ex. 21:12-16; Ex. 22:19-27; Lev. 20:10-21; Deut. 21:18-21)

4) City of refuge for accidental death (Num. 35:1-13).

I explain each of these penalties in *Crime and Punishment: A Biblical Perspective*.[57] While some may think that some of these penalties are harsh, in reality, they were, and are, more humane than any laws created by men. They are the best means of effectively dealing with crime the world has seen, which is only logical as they emanate from the perfect God. On close examination of the biblical penalties, we see that God's mercy is incorporated into God's law, as He is both merciful and just. (The laws must, of course, be applied correctly to see God's great wisdom behind them, and men have often failed to do so. When this has occurred some people have attacked God's law, or God Himself, as unjust, rather than the misapplication of God's good law.)

Tyranny is the fruit of usurpation of authority.

Leaders throughout history have abused authority in doing what they are supposed to do (i.e., in trying to fulfill their divine purpose). The result is tyranny and bondage. But tyranny and bondage are also the result of leaders who mean well, yet are trying to do something outside their jurisdiction. Modern examples in America include:

1) Education — As the state has gained a monopoly in education, and humanism has become the religion of the state, the quality of education has declined, even while costs have sky-rocketed.

2) Welfare state — In the 1960s we launched a war against poverty, and poverty won, even though we have spent trillions of dollars in this area.

Government has assumed a primary role in both of these areas as individuals, families, and churches have given up their responsibilities. Government leaders have failed to see the limited function of civil government.

Limited Government

What is the biblical perspective on the size of civil government? While some Christians argue for big government, the weight of biblical and historical evidence supports limited government.

We have learned that civil government is a divine institution with an important function, but it is to be limited. The power it exercises should only be enough to enable it to fulfill its biblical purpose. Any more and it becomes oppressive and tyrannical. Civil government should not usurp the authority of God or the other divine institutions He established.

Jesus taught that we are to render to God the things that are God's, which is an argument for limited government. The concept of Christian self-government is another strong point supporting limited government because the size of civil government declines as self-government increases (and self-government increases where the Gospel is implanted in the culture). Government is not to control individual conscience. It is not to hinder biblical worship, morality, or action. History shows that centralized power leads to loss of Christian liberty in all spheres of life (religious, political, economic, and civil). That God desires men to live free is another support for small government.

Private property rights are a strong argument for limited government. God created man as His steward (delegated ruler) over the earth (Gen. 1:26-30; Ps. 8:6-8; 1 Cor. 6:3). Man has authority and freedom to manage all the resources God has given him to fulfill his calling (Mt. 25:14-18, 27; Lk. 19:13, 23). The larger the state becomes, the less private property individuals possess (through state ownership and control, as well as increased taxes) and, hence, they have less ability to fulfill the Creation Mandate.[58]

Most arguments for big government involve usurpation of authority, where civil government assumes the responsibilities for charity and other works that the Bible says belong to other institutions.

Government performs a negative, rather than positive, role in society; that is, it punishes men when they violate God's standard of moral behavior (as summarized in the Ten Commandments[59]). This negative role helps limit its power and authority. It protects citizens as they pursue the acquisition of property and knowledge, and maintenance of health and life. It is not to provide property, education, health, or welfare. Acting in a positive way increases its power and in turn diminishes our liberties.

The Bible is full of examples of abusive governments and leaders. Perhaps the best known example is Pharaoh, who refused to release the children of Israel from bondage, even when threatened with God's judgments. The plagues were attempts to change the mind of the totalitarian Egyptian leader so he would act in accordance with God's will. Passover is a celebration of God's work to deliver His people from a bad civil ruler.

With this oppressive example of a monarchial form of government in everyone's mind, Moses, via God's instruction, established a constitutional republic with an executive whose powers were limited and checked by the other elected leaders (see Chapter 8). Unfortunately, God's people rejected His plan for limited government and asked for a king. They tried to do so with Gideon (Judges 8:23), who rebuffed their efforts, but did succeed when Samuel's sons began to govern (1 Sam. 8).

Kings and Big Government

The book of Samuel chapter 8 reveals why the Israelites instituted kings contrary to God's wishes. When Samuel the Judge (Chief Magistrate) was old he appointed his sons as judges over Israel (v. 1). That they were corrupt, unjust,

and did not follow God's law was one reason the people asked Samuel for a king (v. 3). They also wanted to be like all the other nations who had monarchies (v. 5, 20). In addition, they had grown tired of governing themselves and fighting their battles (v. 20), and so a lack of self-government contributed to the establishment of royal rulers.

Both Samuel and the Lord were displeased with the people's request, God declaring that their action indicated they were rejecting Him as their ultimate leader (v. 6-7). God allowed them to set up kings ("I gave you a king in My anger," Hos. 13:11), but He told Samuel to warn them of the grave consequences of a pagan top-down form of government:

Samuel anoints David as king. God allowed the Israelites to set up kings, but He told Samuel to warn them of the grave consequences of a pagan top-down form of government.

> This will be the procedure of the king who will reign over you; he will **take** your sons …. He will **take** your daughters…. He will **take** the best of your fields…. He will **take** a tenth of your seed…. He will also **take** your … best young men … for his work…. He will **take** a tenth of your flocks, and you yourselves will become his servants." (1 Sam. 8:10-18)

Tyrannical governments will take from man what God wants man to have. The consequence of government taking what does not belong to it is enslavement of the people in the nation. If government controls all property it controls all life. It thus robs humans of expressing the image of God and living in the great liberty that God intended for man from the beginning. Statism turns a nation into a giant prison.

Statism is the belief that civil government or the state is the ultimate authority. Statism has many forms: socialism, communism, fascism, democratic socialism, etc. Statism, in essence, elevates man as god, which is the original sin of Adam and Eve. In eating of the tree of the knowledge of good and evil, Adam and Eve declared they would determine for themselves what was good and evil instead of following God's declaration (Gen. 3:5). Man has ever since worshiped himself, but it is via corporate man – i.e. the state – that this has been most devastating to mankind.

Pagan civil governments not only seek to control your external property but also your internal property; that is, your thoughts and ideas. Consider a recent law passed by the city of San Antonio. It forbids anyone who opposes homosexuality from running for office or serving in the government, and you can be fined for holding this position! Tyrannical governments will invade rights of conscience as well as external property rights. The power that can invade liberty of conscience, can also usurp civil liberty. Internal property rights must, therefore, be guarded at all costs, for as they are diminished, every inalienable right of man is jeopardized.

God did not establish government by kings, but when they asked for it He sought to turn Israel from establishing royal government because He knew that kings would "take … take…take" and make citizens serve them. They would take property, children, and freedom, and eventually make the people slaves. Most of Israel's kings acted as God said they would. Even Solomon, who started well, ended by taking (1 Kings 11). Evil kings were worse. The nation of Israel was split in two due to the action of bad rulers. Rehoboam refused to limit his authority and ended up losing half his kingdom (1 Kings 12:14 ff). In His foreknowledge, God required kings to learn and obey His law, which would limit their power and promote just action (Dt. 17:18-20).

The ultimate rebellion of man against God is his embracing and worshiping worldly rulers who claim supreme authority (see the Book of Revelation). Jesus was offered this position when he was tempted at the beginning of His ministry, but He rejected it. When men offer such power to other fallen men, they rarely reject it. History affirms the negative consequences of monarchial rule.

The Jurisdiction of Government

Government's role in society is primarily to protect the life, liberty, and property of people. It restrains and punishes evil-doers. A society cannot tolerate all behavior (even all behavior among consenting adults), therefore, crimes against property, life, and restriction of biblical liberty must be punished in accordance with God's law. In general, governments restrict the ungodly external civil action of men, rather than internal thoughts and ideology of men.

However, this does not mean governments should allow the dissemination of all ideas, because many ideas undermine the life, liberty, and property of others as well as the security and existence of the nation at large. Treasonous words (calling for the destruction of the state) can be punished. Teaching immoral ideas leads to living immorally; therefore, there is a place for obscenity laws.

Toleration of all actions and ideas is not biblical freedom. Promoting child molestation is wrong and criminal. Promoting theft and murder is wrong and criminal.

The secular view of liberty is that man is free to do whatever he wants to do. In contrast, Christian liberty is freedom to do what God wants us to do. Secular liberty is detached from truth. In practice, such secularists tolerate anything except Christianity since it adheres to truth and exposes their wrong thinking and action. To them, it is a crime to deny total liberty. Relativism will seek to destroy every trace of Christianity in the public (and eventually private) life of a nation. This is occurring in America and many nations today. Relativism is the new religion and it will not tolerate contrary religions. Intolerance to secularists' "liberty to do all" religion is the one major crime; hence, Christian truth is criminal – it is the highest heresy. However, since biblical Christianity is rooted in truth, there is only liberty for mankind under God's law.

Law (and liberty) rests upon truth. Law is concerned with right and wrong. Governments should enforce laws against wrong behavior and promotion of wrong behavior. Governments cannot discern motives (hence, hate crimes are unbiblical) and should not punish motives, but they can evaluate actions and ideas. If truth is removed from civil government, all that remains is simply power or coercion. No internal unity of ideas exists to unite the people in a civil union. Truth must restrain the power of the state. Without truth as a restraint, civil government grows in its power and control over all things. To the relativist all truth is opinion, and for their correct "truth" to prevail they must obtain power via government to enforce "truth." Coercion is the fundamental basis for secular society.

When civil government is separated from truth, its power grows. For a season men will have a license to live as they wish, all the while their liberty is being taken from them by an ever-growing state. Understanding the pagan nature of man, John Cotton declared, "It is necessary…that all power on earth be limited."[60]

Comparing Christian and Humanistic Views of Government

We have seen that the Bible teaches that civil government is a divine institution that has an important but limited role in society. Governments exist to protect the property of people (see Chapter 7 on the principle of property). Yet, due to the fallen nature of man, most governments throughout history have not protected the property of people but plundered them. The French economist, statesman, and author Frederic Bastiat (1801-1850) explains this well in his classic book *The Law*.

Frederic Bastiat

Humanistic governments will usurp the authority of individuals, the family, and the church. Usurpation is exercising authority that does not belong to you. Whenever usurpation of power occurs, liberty is diminished and all sorts of problems arise.

The following charts present various conceptions of society (and the role of civil government), including biblical, statist, secular, and religious statist. Structuring society in a biblical manner will produce the most liberty, prosperity, order, and justice, as well as enable man to best fulfill his purpose to bring God's kingdom to earth.

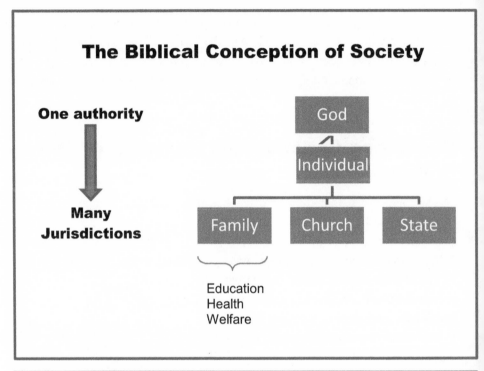

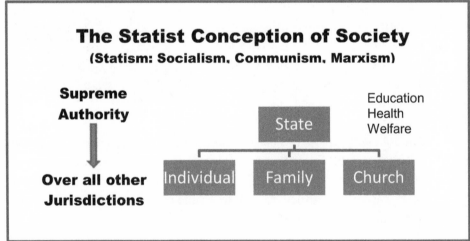

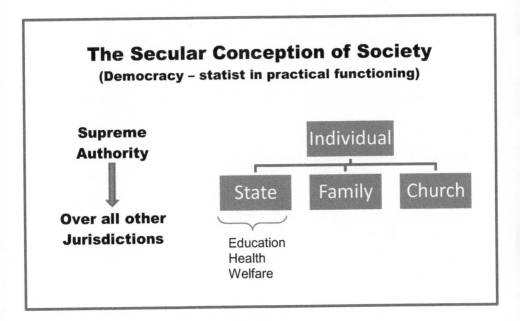

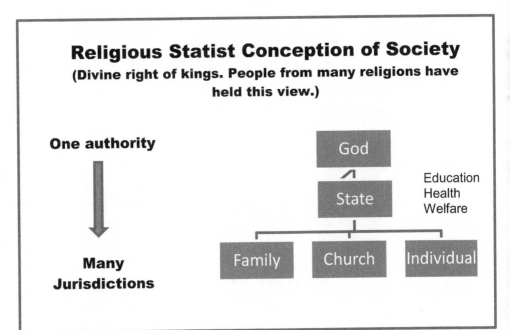

The flow of power in a Christian society is from the inside-out. The flow of power in a pagan society is from the outside-in, from the top-down. This top-down flow occurs because the people see the rulers as the source of power and authority — they are the ultimate authority in the earth. However, the state is not man's savior, nor is it the ultimate authority in the earth. Caesar thought he was, but Jesus made clear his authority was from God and was limited (see Chapter 5). Most leaders throughout history have had this Caesar mentality, with most citizens agreeing. The spread of Christian ideas, especially after the Protestant Reformation, changed this in many nations, but, unfortunately, a majority of these nations are moving back toward a pagan view of government. Many people in the United States are embracing this idea as well. When trouble comes, who do people look to for help, provision, and "salvation"? Many first look to civil government, thinking the government owes them this provision. Many in the media agree and often lambaste the government if it is not acting fast enough, being efficient, or providing enough relief. (Since it is not the purpose of civil government to provide all things for the citizens, it will never do this effectively or efficiently.)

Secularists have no savior, so they often look to government to be their savior — to bring peace, to establish a utopia, to meet needs, to provide material things, and so on. Christians have a Savior and do not need government for this. From a Christian perspective, civil government is a divine institution with a legitimate function, but it is very limited in what it is supposed to do. It is to protect the righteous, punish the evil doer, and administer God's justice in the civil realm that is under its sphere of authority.

The Christian idea of government teaches that the state exists to serve man, not vice versa; that government flows from the internal to the external, from the bottom-up; that government begins with self-government, then flows to the family, church, and the civil realm.

Statism can provide security (in a small degree) but at the price of liberty. Living by faith in Christ requires trusting Him. The free man lives in a world of free enterprise, trial and error, profit and loss, success and failure. The free man must walk by faith. It is not easy to walk by faith and to do so requires a living faith in God. Having faith in the state to provide for you takes away your liberty. It may provide some security, but that is a dependent security, being a slave of the state.

Comparing Christian and Humanistic Views of Government and Law

The following chart summarizes some of the ideas presented previously contrasting a Christian versus a humanistic view of government.

Christian	Humanistic
Begins with internal self-government	Begins with external civil government
Restrained by Truth of God's Word	Restrained only by sense of rulers own self-restraint
Power limited by constitution, people, checks and balances	Ever increasing power and coercion
People and rulers under law of God	People and rulers over law or apart from law
Liberty – free to do God's will	Liberty – free to do whatever one wants
Government protects property of citizens	Government plunders property of citizens
The state is a minister of God.	The state is god walking upon the earth. (Hegel)
Jesus is Savior.	Government is savior.

Contrast of Biblical and Humanistic View of Law

Government and law are closely connected since civil governments are involved in making, executing, and judging law. Law, from a Christian perspective and as the Founders of America viewed it, originates in the will of God, revealed in general to man through nature and his conscience, and more specifically in the revelation of the Scriptures. Law from a humanistic view is rooted in man, ultimately autonomous man, but practically in the state, and in the consensus of the majority, or of a powerful minority.

From a biblical perspective man is fallen and fallible, has a sinful nature, and thus needs to be restrained. The biblical purpose of civil law is to restrain the evil action of men in society. True law reveals what is right and wrong, and hence, exposes law-breakers. But law in itself cannot produce what is right, it cannot change the heart or attitude of man, therefore, the Christian acknowledges the inability to legislate good, or to make people moral by passing laws. However, the Christian recognizes the moral basis of all laws. All laws everywhere are based upon the moral presuppositions of the law-makers. Laws against murder reflect a moral belief. Laws against theft are based upon the command to not steal. All law has a moral concern. The important question to the Christian is "whose morality does it legislate?"

From a Christian presupposition then, the law cannot change or reform man; this is a spiritual matter. Man can only be changed by the grace of God. He cannot be legislated into a new morality.

Humanists see the evils in society and in man, but explain them differently than Christians. To the humanist there is no higher being than man. There is no incarnate Savior. From a humanistic perspective there is no hope of internal regeneration to save man, therefore, any salvation or transformation that occurs in men or nations must come from man. Historically, humanistic man has tended to use the instrument of law and government to attempt to bring such a transformation or "salvation."

Having no other means of provision, of salvation, or of peace, humanistic man attempts to regulate and provide all things through government and law. It is only through the force of law that evil will be eliminated and utopia established on earth. Humanistic law is used to promote and advance humanistic morals. Such law, in conjunction with a corresponding educational system, is the only hope humanistic man has of establishing a "saved" or "righteous" — that is, good and progressing — society.

To restate this, if there is no God who redeems man internally, then any elimination of problems brought on by what is in the heart of man must be done by man — often collective man and his government. The attempt will thus be made by government (at least those that have a vision for a progressing society) to use the instrument of law to bring more peace and goodwill among men and to eliminate all that is negative, such as poverty, crime, war, disease, prejudice, and ignorance.

From a Christian perspective, law can restrain sinful man from acting wickedly, for the fear of punishment is a deterrent, but he cannot be changed by law. Unless the evil heart of man is changed, there will be no advancement toward a better society. Humanistic law seeks to save and change man internally. Since the government (and laws issued thereby) is the instrument for such change, the government becomes the savior in a humanistic society.

Therefore, there is a great potential for the humanist to see law (and the state from which it comes) as savior. This might not be overtly proclaimed, but is demonstrated by actions. Certainly man is the highest authority and the source of law in a humanistic society, and hence he is the god of that society, for the source of law of a society is the god of a society — and man will look to his god to assist him, to provide for him, and to save him.

The founders of America, who had a predominantly Christian worldview, saw God, through His Son Jesus, as their savior. The state served a legitimate but limited purpose to protect the life, liberty, and property of the citizens. From a Christian perspective the state is limited. The United States Constitution, as well as the various state constitutions, is based upon the Christian idea that man is sinful and cannot be entrusted with too much power because his tendency is to abuse governmental power. The very limited functions of the national government are listed in this document, with a system of checks and balances as a further curb on abuse. In addition, governing officials are regularly held accountable to the people through elections. As stated previously, John Adams clearly understood the need to limit the power of those who govern due to original sin, writing:

> There is no man so blind as not to see, that to talk of founding a government upon a supposition that nations and great bodies of men, left to themselves, will practice a course of self-denial, is either to babble like a new-born infant, or to deceive like an unprincipled impostor.[61]

John Adams said "the heart is deceitful above all things, and desperately wicked."

There are people with a humanistic view of law who are for limited government. However, in nations that have embraced a humanistic view of law, the state generally acts as the sovereign, where all spheres of life come under its authority and direction (for example, ancient Rome, the former U.S.S.R., and present day China). Similarly, there have been nations that have verbally embraced a Christian view of law but did not practice limited government. But those who founded America would argue that correct and consistent Christian thought would produce limited and free government. The history of America is a great confirmation of this.

Thus, one reason a people's view of law is important is that it affects the scope and extent of civil government in a nation. It also affects the form of government.

The source and origin of law has to do with sovereignty, with ultimate authority, with a people's view of "God," for the source of law of a society is the god of that society. A people's religion, by which is meant their ultimate source of authority, determines their view of law and everything else.

What relationship should there be between church and state, or God and government?

The Scriptures teach that God ordained the state, as well as the church and family, and gave each of these divine institutions certain responsibilities and powers. There is a separation of their jurisdictions. The state should not usurp the authority of the church or the family. The church should not usurp the authority of the state or the family, and the family should not usurp the authority of the other two divine institutions. This is the biblical meaning of the phrase "separation of church and state." The state has limited power and should not encroach upon the authority and purpose of the church.

If church and state are to be separated jurisdictionally, then what relation should there be between the church and state in a nation? As institutions, the church, state, and family must be separated, but we should not separate God from government. In fact we cannot separate God from government any more than we can separate God from the family. God created the family (Gen. 2-3) and God created government (Gen. 9:6; Rom. 13:1-4). Since God created and is sovereign over civil government (John 19:11), it is impossible to separate God from government.

All nations are built upon some religion.

While many governments do not acknowledge God, they, nonetheless, have their foundation in religion or the faith of the people. The predominant faith or worldview held by the citizens dictates a basic morality which will be reflected by those who govern the nation and make the laws. So all governments, and laws that flow from them, are built upon some religion or worldview which provides the basis for right and wrong behavior in society.

Who is the source of law in a society?

The source of law in a society is the god of that society. If the Bible is the source of law, of what is right and wrong behavior— of what is lawful and unlawful — then the God of the Bible is the god of that society. If man is the source of law, where a majority or ruling minority determines what is right and wrong, then man is the god of that society (this is secular humanism).

The source of law and morality in America has been the Christian religion, though this has been changing as Christians have retreated from influencing culture. Christianity has produced ideas and principles fundamental to freedom. Things such as not stealing, not committing murder, and honest dealings with others come from the Bible. We do not want to separate such biblical principles from government. If we do, the result will be anarchy or tyranny.

We, also, do not want to separate the church from teaching such principles. The pastor and church have the duty to teach Christians everything Christ commanded them, including teachings that relate to the family and the state. The church has authority to speak the truth to all institutions in society — the church is "the pillar and foundation of the truth" (1 Tim. 3:15). In terms of speaking the truth, it must not be separate from the family or the state. The church must inform them, for the church builds the people, and the people build the nation.

The Relation of God and Government

How then should God and government relate? For a nation to be great it needs the Spirit of God and the Law/Word of God (Deut. 4:5-8). Therefore, a government and its laws should be built upon God's higher law (i.e., it has the Law/Word of God), and rulers should be Christian and uphold God's law (it has the presence of God). Both of these, of course, are dependent upon the citizens first displaying these characteristics.

1. Government and laws should be built upon God's higher law.

Proverbs says, "Happy is he who keeps the law." This is true of men and nations. Civil rulers, or judges, are to be ministers of God for good (Rom. 13). They are to judge for God. They are to represent God more so than the people. As the civil leader of Israel, Moses made "known the statutes of God and His laws" (Ex. 18:16). This is how he judged in disputes between people. "God filled the civil officers of Israel with His Spirit, to signify that they were prophets of God, called to speak for God in the ministry of justice (Num. 11:16)."[62]

America's form of government and her system of laws were built upon God's higher law. One of thousands of examples of this can be seen in the document which was the precursor of the Bill of Rights, the Massachusetts Body of Liberties, written by Rev. Nathaniel Ward in 1641. The Pentateuch was the basis for its criminal code, and "in case of the defect of a law in any partecular case" the standard was "the word of God."[63] The Word of God is the law of liberty (Jam. 2:12). God's Word is the standard for law that will make men free.

After all, the Bible, according to John Calvin, is God's scepter by which He rules His universe. He expects men to take up this scepter wherever they

govern. All men and institutions are under
God's authority and God's Word. All leaders
are bound by the law of God, as the Bible
makes readily clear (Pr. 16:12; Mt. 14:4; 2
Sam. 12:1-14; 1 Ki. 12:31- 13:10).

**2. Rulers should be Christian and uphold
God's law.**

We will examine the qualifications for
biblical leaders in Chapter 10 and see these
include knowledge, morality (Christian
character), and true faith (fear of God) (Ex.
18:21; Deut. 1:13). There is a prophetic
nature to the civil office. "Every reformation
in Israel involved in part a return to the
prophetic nature of the civil office."[64] True
biblical revival not only involves reformation
of the church but also reformation of the
state.

John Calvin said that the Bible
is the scepter by which God
rules His universe.

We need biblical leaders in government. Such leaders are much more than
men who merely go to church or teach Sunday school or vote for prayer in
public schools. Biblical leaders are men full of the presence and law–word of
God, ministering His justice in the civil realm. Such civil leaders should
covenant (or agree) to rule under God's ultimate authority in the manner He
prescribes in His Word. This was God's intent for the leaders of His covenant
nation of Israel (See Chapter 8).

Chapter 7

Seven Foundational Governmental Principles

The Power and Form of Godly Government

Forms of government are important. God gave ancient Israel a unique form of government that would best enable His people to live in liberty, progress, and fulfill their divine purpose. We will examine the form of what E.C. Wines aptly called the Hebrew Republic in the next chapter. While the form was important, it was not sufficient. Without a knowledge of God's Law, a reverential fear of God, and a heart of obedience, Israel could not uphold the godly form of government. They needed a godly power within them to support the godly form of government.

External forms always result from an internal power. This is true for civil governments, churches, homes, businesses, or associations. The power, which is internal, precedes the form, which is external.

Both a power and a form are needed for anything to function properly. The internal power is the life or energizing force and is essential for any form to work as it should; yet, a form is absolutely necessary to channel the power properly. We not only need power and form, but we also need a balance between the two. Too much form causes all involved to dry up, while too much power causes them to "blow up." Communism, for example, produces a form of civil government that relies almost totally on external pressure to keep everyone "in line." The internal creativity, life, and motivation of each individual is suppressed and often dries up by these external constraints. An over-emphasis on power – where the autonomy of every individual is emphasized – leads to anarchy and eventually bondage. Historically, this can be seen after many national revolutions, the French being an excellent example.

In Chapters 8 and 9 we will examine the form of a biblical (and hence, free) government. The principles examined in this section reveal the power of such a government. The form of a Christian government can only come forth and be maintained by a people that have the proper power or spirit within them. Without this foundation, a free government can never be established or maintained. It is not enough for a nation to copy some external form of government to secure liberty. That external form must flow out of the principles of liberty within the heart of the people. The pathway to liberty within a nation is from the internal to the external.

The power and form of Christian nations.

The following principles form the foundation of strong, free, and prosperous individuals, families, churches, businesses, and governments. The Bible teaches and history confirms that the foundational principles of a free society flow out of Christianity. To the degree that nations have applied the principles of the Bible in all spheres of life is the degree to which those nations have prospered and been free.

1. Self-Government

As noted earlier, government begins internally with man learning how to govern himself. Self-government is most fully realized by being subject to God and His commandments. Since living in accordance with His truth is the foundation for free, just, and prosperous societies, Christian self-government is necessary for the future well-being of our nation. The Father of the U.S. Constitution, James Madison, agreed, writing in Federalist #39 of "that honourable determination which animates every votary of freedom, to rest all our political experiments on the capacity of mankind for self-government."[65]

The basis of the ability for man to govern himself well is rooted in his being in subjection to a higher power – to "the Laws of Nature and of Nature's God," as expressed in the U.S. Declaration of Independence. If men do not govern themselves under God, they will be governed externally by force. In the words of the founder of Pennsylvania William Penn, "those people who are not governed by God will be ruled by tyrants."[66]

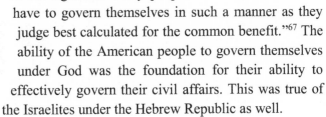

William Penn

One "essential ingredient in the happiness we enjoy as a nation," according to President of the Continental Congress (1782-83) Elias Boudinot, "is the right that every people have to govern themselves in such a manner as they judge best calculated for the common benefit."[67] The ability of the American people to govern themselves under God was the foundation for their ability to effectively govern their civil affairs. This was true of the Israelites under the Hebrew Republic as well.

Elias Boudinot

Consent of the Governed

The principle of self-government implies that people should have a voice in the enactment of laws—they should consent to them. The Hebrew people consented to the laws of God (which was their Constitution) under which they were to live (Ex. 19:8). Their adoption of the Laws of Moses was repeated at the death of Moses and, by a statute, was to be agreed to every seven years at a national convention of the general assembly—the representatives of the people (for consent see Ex. 24:3-8; Dt. 29:9-13; Josh. 8:30-35; Josh. 24; Neh. 8:18; 9:38; 10:1-29). Hence, the government of Israel was a government of the people. Today, individuals must know and consent to the constitution of the nation, which means it must be taught to all citizens and immigrants (and to be effective, the constitution must be based upon biblical law).

As people in a nation become less self-governed, and give up power, the civil government (especially the national government) will grow and grow, making more and more laws (many outside its realm of jurisdiction) and spending more and more money. Lack of self-government leads to greater centralized external government which results in loss of individual liberty.

2. Union or Covenant

The people of a free nation will not only be self-governed but will also voluntarily work in union with each other for the common good of the entire nation. Voluntary union comes from unity of belief.

Most civil unions throughout history have been a result of centralization via political force and military might rather than voluntary consent. Christianity provided the basis of a "community united, not by external bonds, but by the vital force of distinctive ideas and principles."[68] Civil covenants started in America in 1620 when English Pilgrims drew up the Mayflower Compact. They were able to covenant to live together in civil society because some years earlier they had covenanted to join themselves together in a church estate. In fact, American constitutionalism (which has affected constitutions in most nations) is based upon the biblical idea of covenant.

The Bible is full of covenants between man and man and between God and man. The covenant that God makes with men through the atoning work of Jesus Christ is the beginning of the internal heart change necessary for the foundation of freedom in an individual and in a nation. Biblical marriage covenants keep marriages together and strong. Without strong families, no nation can long endure.

The external union of a people results from an internal unity of ideas and principles residing in the hearts of the people. Compulsory union, that imposed by external force and fear, will never last. Union cannot be forced externally, but must arise from internal unity. An understanding of the foundations and framework of a free government must be inculcated in the hearts of all the people for a nation to remain together in union.

Covenant or compact among people on a local level is the basis of political union. For people to covenant together, they must share common beliefs, purposes, ideas, and faith. Joining together for civil purposes begins with covenanting together for independent purposes, such as in homes, churches, schools, clubs, and various organizations. Union is also seen in the commercial realm in partnerships and corporations. Independent and commercial unions not only benefit the people directly involved, but also the general populace. If there is not unity with union on the independent and commercial levels, there can be no political union.

Stronger internal bonds within a people will produce a stronger union. Belief in the One and only true God is the source of unity with union. Christian union is "that oneness of hearts, opinions, and manners, which forms the strongest bond of society."[69] Many factors in how God ordered the nation of Israel contributed to a strong union. One, the general distribution of property to all families produced a general material equality (although the productivity would vary greatly based upon labor, thrift, and wisdom). Two, education for all also contributed to the national union as everyone held a common worldview rooted in the Word of God. Three, godly morality was also a factor. The Commandments teach us how to love our neighbor – protect their life, liberty, property, family, and reputation (the Second Table, Commandments 6-10) – and also command us to love the stranger (Ex. 23:9). God Himself demonstrates love and service among the Godhead, and we are to imitate Him. All of these factors promote a

---

Union or Covenant

The external union of a people results from an internal unity of ideas and principles residing in the hearts of the people.

Unity with Union

⬇   ⬇

Internal   External

The church should supply the unifying ideas.

friendship, love, and equality among the people. Ubiquitous education, property rights, and morality will contribute to strong unions in nations today.[70]

The strongest force for unity and union is the common belief that God is over all, and all men have equal standing before Him and His law. All men, being created in His image, have equal civil rights that are rooted in the Ten Commandments. The idea of biblical equality under God's law discounted caste systems and gave rise historically to the idea of a Declaration of Rights. Christian union makes nations strong.

The application of the principle of union in the various levels of government will allow them to work together for the good of all, while self-government in the people will assure that the rights of individuals are maintained as well. The principles of self-government and union must be kept in balance. Too much emphasis on union will result in centralism, while too much emphasis on self-government leads to disintegration of the nation.

3. Individuality

The principle of individuality reveals that each person is created by God and is unique and distinct. Each has a well-defined existence with unique talents and abilities which fits him for a special purpose. All men are alike in many ways (there is a unity among mankind), yet no two men are alike (there is also diversity). Man has physical characteristics that make him unique, such as his fingerprints, profile, voiceprints, scent, and nerve pattern on the inside of the eye. He also has unique internal characteristics, including thoughts, opinions, emotions, and attitudes.

Man is a reflection of his Creator, who is a unity (God is One), yet He is also diverse (God is a triune Being). God does not create carbon-copy molds of anything, whether humans, animals, trees, minerals, mountains, rivers, planets or stars. Everything He creates is unique and distinct, yet there is a unity among all things for God created them all.

Every person has his own outward and inward identity or individuality. Every person is responsible and accountable for his own choices and actions. For governments to be free, the people must assume this responsibility. Everyone must also recognize the value of life.

Life is valuable because man is created in the image of God (Gen. 1:26-28). The sanctity of human life is taught throughout the Bible. God's laws protect innocent life. Willful murder was punished by death (Num. 35: 33).

Men were required to build a fence or protective barrier around their roofs to protect others from potential harm (Deut. 22:8). Unlike most other nations, Hebrew parents had no authority to take the life of their children. Action to purge the land had to be taken by civil authorities in a community if a homicide by an unknown person took place (Deut. 21:1-9).[71]

Man, being created by God with a unique existence, has an independent value. His value is not dependent upon his ability to contribute to the state. Man is of highest value and the state exists to serve man, rather than man serve the state. Man, therefore, is superior to the state. In a government that views the state as paramount, individuals' lives, liberty, and property will be in danger if they do not cooperate with or contribute to the state.

The principle of individuality further reveals that all men are equal. However, men are not equal in their talents and abilities, but they are equal in their right to life, liberty and the pursuit of acquiring property. Governments embodying false ideas of equality say men have an equal right to material possessions and thus try to distribute the wealth accordingly. All men have equal rights before the law. Governments exist in order to secure those rights.

A free government will keep a balance of unity with diversity. Too much emphasis on diversity leads to anarchy or freedom run wild. In such a state man will be self-centered, and lawlessness, license, and nihilism will be predominant. The resulting forms of government will run from anarchy to pure democracy.

Tyranny will result from an over-emphasis on unity. The rulers (or ruler) will center in on themselves and do as they please for their benefit or what they consider to be of benefit to the whole. The result is centralization of power leading to slavery and bondage to large groups of people. The forms of government that result from this mentality range from bureaucracy or collectivism (socialism, communism) to dictatorship. Here, the central government determines the rights and liberties of the people.

A balance of unity and diversity will produce liberty with order in a society and government by the consent of the governed. The resulting form of government will be a decentralized, democratic constitutional republic.

4. Property or Conscience

A person's property is whatever he has exclusive right to possess and control. Property is first internal. A person's conscience is his most precious aspect of property because it tells him what is right and wrong in his actions. Each person in a free government must be a good steward of his conscience and keep it clear. By doing so, he will know what is right and wrong from within and, therefore, he will be able to live his life in a right manner. The apostle Paul said he did his "best to maintain always a blameless conscience both before God and before men" (Acts 24:16).

How one takes care of his internal property will determine how he takes care of his external property. The following chart reveals various aspects of internal and external property:

Internal Property	External Property
Thoughts	Land/Estate
Opinions	Money
Talents	Freedom of Speech
Conscience	Bodily Health
Ideas	Possessions
Mind	Freedom of Assembly
Affections	

The idea of property is so important to God that three of His Ten Commandments protect property rights (commandments 6, where life is a form of property, 8, and 10). Much of the Mosaic Law (and the Bible in general) deals with obtaining, increasing, protecting, and distributing property (both internal and external). There can be no civil society without private ownership of property (including land, clothes, tools, homes, weapons). People will not willingly till the land if others have an equal right to the harvest, nor will they build a home if another can take possession of it when it is finished. When the lazy receive as much as the diligent, then the motivation to develop character qualities necessary for freedom and prosperity – like industry, thrift, frugality, and inventiveness – will be lost. Socialism and all forms of statism reward behavior contrary to God's Word, and consequently, do not produce a growing and free society, but rather a stagnant nation full of indolent and ignorant men.

Property rights are the basis for political equality. In ancient Israel all citizens were members of the body politic and had a voice in government. Their power and voice was derived from their ownership of land/property. Each family in ancient Israel was given a share of the land that they owned, managed, and cultivated, and this was inviolable (or made permanent) as the land was returned to the original owners in the Year of Jubilee (every 50 years), and in the Sabbath (seventh) year debts were forgiven and slaves were set free. These provisions also helped preserve the family, enabling the Israelites to retain their family holdings.

E.C. Wines writes, "Property in the soil is the natural foundation of power, and consequently of authority."[72] If ownership of the property in a nation is dispersed among all men, they will not be enslaved to a few powerful land owners. As Noah Webster said: "Let the people have property and they will have power."[73] If they have power, then they will have control of the state. Their power is not conferred upon them by the state or aristocracy. "The men who own the territory of a state will exercise a predominating influence over the public affairs of such state."[74] Property not only includes land, but also businesses, manufacturing, and various other means of producing goods and services.

The distribution of land to all families in ancient Israel had a number of positive consequences: 1) It made extreme poverty and huge wealth impossible. It kept the rich from accumulating large land holdings, and forming an elite class. 2) Everyone had an interest in maintaining peace and order in society so they could fully cultivate their land, and therefore, they had an interest in being involved in governmental affairs. 3) It promoted industry and frugality, as these are needed to cultivate property. 4) It enabled everyone to have a degree of independence, as they could provide for their own household. They did not have to look to government, or someone else, to provide for them. At the same time, the government protected everyone's right to property. If you found yourself in poverty, you could not blame someone else.

God did not intend for the government of Israel, or of any nation, to provide material goods to the citizens. Governments do not exist to provide property; rather, governments exist to protect property of every sort, most importantly, liberty of conscience. Tyrannical governments will invade rights of conscience as well as external property rights. The power that can invade liberty of conscience, can also usurp civil liberty. Internal property rights must, therefore, be guarded at all costs, for as they are diminished, every inalienable right of man is jeopardized.

The famous British political scientist, John Locke, wrote in his treatise *Of Civil Government*:

For Men being the Workmanship of one Omnipotent, and infinitely wise Maker: All the Servants of one Sovereign Master, sent into the World by His Order, and about His Business, they are His Property, whose Workmanship they are, made to last during His, not one anothers Pleasure.[75]

John Locke

Locke goes on to state that while we are God's property, God has given us the responsibility to be good stewards over our persons. He wrote that "every man has a Property in his own Person." It follows we have a God-given right to everything necessary to preserve our persons, to internal and external property.

In other words, God has created everything, including us, and given us the right to possess internal and external property. God requires us to be good stewards of everything He puts into our hand, whether that be houses, land, and money (external property) or talents, abilities, and knowledge (internal property). The idea of stewardship is embodied in the principle of property.

Before any property can be taken from us, we must give our consent. If our property can be taken without our consent, then we really have no property. This is why any taxes imposed by a government on its citizens must be done by elected representatives. We give our consent to taxes or laws affecting our property rights through our representatives. If they do not represent our views, we should work to replace them in a lawful manner.

A people standing on the principle of property will take action to prohibit government or other citizens from taking anyone's personal property without their consent, or from violating anyone's conscience and rights. Lack of this principle in the lives of citizens will lead to unjust taxation, a government controlled economy, and usurpation of both internal and external property rights.

One reason that property is valuable is due to its potential productivity. Agricultural production is primary as this is the foundation of prosperous and happy nations. Israel was represented as a land flowing with milk and honey, a land of wheat, barley, vines, and fig trees, and in many other similar terms of abundance (Ex. 3:8; Deut. 1:25; 8:7-10). Every family and those born to the families would inherit a portion of this rich land. Food production is foundational for any nation. Without being able to meet the basic needs of the people, a nation cannot grow and advance.

Agriculture has many positive influences for individuals and the nation at large. It produces character, industry, frugality, physical stamina, and rugged independence – traits necessary to live in liberty. It strengthens a love for the country while providing the necessities of life. It also helps keep peace because men will not use the sword as an aggressor, but only in defense of his property, if that need arises.

Pagans view manual labor as demeaning and for the lower class. Pagan nations have sought to enslave others to labor for them in the fields. In contrast, Moses (following God's instruction) regarded agriculture as the most honorable of employments. Elisha was ploughing the fields when he was called by Elijah. David was taken from the sheepfold to become king. Moses, himself, was called from a pastoral life to free God's people.

Godly leaders should honor agriculture and enact laws to support men as they work their fields. Laws should encourage a general ownership of property among citizens. (This was so in early America and was one reason for her great prosperity and equality.) The land should be owned by those who till it. Such ownership produces industry, as well as mental and muscular vigor. It gives people power. Most political evils in history have resulted from "the unrighteous monopoly of the earth."[76] Therefore, land and farms (as well as other forms of property) should be dispersed widely among the people. God's plan for Israel did this.

Labor

Labor was elevated to a high place under the Hebrew Republic and is encouraged throughout the Bible. Labor is the title deed to property; it is necessary to be productive. Land ownership promotes labor in all citizens. Paul writes, "If any man will not work, neither shall he eat" (2 Thess. 3:10). Owning land promoted work and hence, adherence to Paul's exhortation. Labor is both physical and intellectual. The Hebrew society rested upon labor.

Industry of all citizens is needed for freedom and prosperity. God's people were to labor to cultivate the land and build houses, so that they could eat and be satisfied and dwell comfortably in their homes (Prov. 24:27; Deut. 8:12 – while doing this they were not to forget God). Their labor also produced many agricultural and clothing products, pottery, metal workings, furniture, musical instruments, roads, engravings, buildings, and many other things to make man's life more comfortable and enjoyable. Their labor did not, however, produce monuments to leaders. This was typically done by pagan nations and almost always with slave labor (such as the Egyptian pyramids and Roman Colosseum). There were not slaves in Israel to produce such structures, and "free labor employs itself about things more useful."[77]

Daniel Webster said (as summarized by Wine), "if it was for his sins that man was condemned to till the ground, it was the most merciful judgment that almighty benignity could have inflicted upon him."[78] In God's judgment upon man to till the ground with sweat and labor was the seed of his preservation, because his labor produced the character and ability to manage property necessary to survive while God brought forth the Messiah and new creation man.

5. Education — Sowing and Reaping

An ignorant people will quickly become a people enslaved. Only a well-instructed citizenry can be permanently free. To preserve liberty in a nation, the general populace must understand the principles upon which a free government is based, for as they do, they will be able to prevent the leaders from eroding their constitutional rights and protections.

Education of all people is a biblical idea. In the Hebrew Republic, everyone was required to know God's laws—the constitution—and the history of the nation. An ignorant people cannot be a free people. Education in the duties and actions of free societies is essential. Parents were to teach their children the law and history every day (Deut. 6:7). The festivals, commemorative rites, and holy days that God implemented were a regular means of educating the people (Ex. 13:14-15). These included the Passover, Pentecost, the feast of tabernacles, and the monumental heap of stones at Gilgal.[79]

Hebrew parents taught their children orally God's word and works, but they also taught them to read and write. They were commanded to write God's law. The Hebrew people had a level of literacy that surpassed any nation of antiquity.[80] This was true during New Testament times as well. Jesus often said to the people: "Have you not read?" (Matt. 12:3; 19:4; 21:16; 22:31; Mark 2:25; 12:10, 26; Luke 6:3). They had the ability to examine the Scriptures for themselves, which is essential for free nations. Since the time of Christ, this biblical mandate has been especially embraced in societies where biblical Christianity has had a great influence, America being the foremost example.

After the parents, the Levites were the primary educators in Israel because they were the most knowledgeable of God's law. During the reformation of Jehoshaphat, the priests went throughout the land and taught the people the laws of Moses (2 Chron. 17:8-9). (See Chapter 8 for more on the educational role of the Levites.)

Schools of the prophets were established as seminaries of higher learning (1 Sam. 19:18-24; 2 Kings 2:3, 5) where men studied the law and learned to discern God's will. More than merely a place to learn the art of prophecy, they taught the truth of God's Word as it applied to all of life. Most early colleges in America and Christian Europe were founded with this same goal in mind.

The Mosaic system of education prepared every man to fulfill his calling in both his particular business and his general business. Biblical education prepares man for his vocation — his particular business where he provides a needed good or service to mankind and in so doing provides for his own needs and those of his family — as well as his general calling — his general business of being able to live in liberty by fulfilling his biblical duties in family, church, and civil society. To establish a free, peaceful, and advancing society, all people must understand and perform their duties in both personal and public affairs. God's Word prepares them for this, but it must be taught to each generation.

The Bible (and especially the Mosaic Law) teaches that everyone should be educated. It is for all people regardless of rank and conditions, which is in great contrast to the view of most nations throughout history where only the high class and wealthy had access to instruction. The prevalence of this pagan idea prohibited liberty from advancing. As the Christian idea of education – that every citizen should know the law and truth – advanced, liberty advanced with it. Biblical truth includes political knowledge as well as moral knowledge. This knowledge motivates the common man to resist the rise of arbitrary power and encroachment upon their God-given rights and liberties.

Biblical education develops both the inward and outward man. It transforms the manners and habits of youth, as well as instructs in personal and political rights and duties. The fruit of such education is great virtue, liberty, prosperity, and peace. Education was so important to God that He set aside an entire tribe (the Levites) for worship and instruction. They were not to possess a monopoly of the truth (which pagan man tends to do) but pass it on to the general populace. The well-being of the nation depended upon it.

Education is a sowing and reaping process. It is like a seed. The Bible tells us much about the "seed principle." It is extremely important for us to understand the parable of the sower and the soils (Mark 4), and that the kingdom of God is like a seed. Although we are instantly converted when we repent and submit ourselves to Christ, the establishment of God's character and kingdom within us is a gradual process. It takes place like the growth of a plant or tree. A seed is planted; nourishment, care, and sunlight are provided; and then a mature plant comes forth bearing fruit (we must remember the pruning process, also).

This same principle applies in establishing God's truth in the nations of the world. It is a gradual process that must occur in one way through Christian education. The ideas that are sown in a people will grow over the years and produce fruit, manifesting in every aspect of life — personal, social, political, economic. That is why the philosophy of the schools in one generation will be the philosophy of government in the next.

What the educational institutions of a country teach lays the foundation for liberty or bondage, depending upon the ideas imparted. Education is the means for propagating a governmental philosophy. In recent times, where Marxists have taken over certain countries, one of the first things they have done is to assume control of the educational system and through that teach their ideologies and propagate their ideas.

Every government has its own philosophy of education. Public educational institutions will always teach the philosophy of the state. This is one reason why most education should be kept in the private sector. If government or public schools exist, efforts should be taken to keep them decentralized and controlled on the local level. If the educational philosophy of a nation is changed, the governmental philosophy will change in the future.

For a free government to be sustained, the people must have an understanding of the working and structure of free government. The people can then keep an enlightened eye on their civil leaders. However, education involves more than just acquiring knowledge or learning facts. Of greater importance is education in morals and principles. We have seen that the citizens of a nation that desire to be free and prosperous must be people of principle. Education in the Christian religion and morality is of first importance. Such education should not merely impart knowledge of morality, but actually implant morals and virtue within the people. The godly characteristics that are almost universally accepted as fundamental for free and stable societies all have their roots in the Bible, and include such things as honesty, loyalty, diligence, and concern for others.

True education is the means for propagating free government to future generations. Without it, tyranny will reign. Biblical education forms a wise and virtuous public opinion. The ultimate check upon tyranny rests in an enlightened and moral people.

6. Morality or Christian Character

No nation can long endure without virtue or morality in the people. A loss of principles and manners is the greatest threat to a free people and will cause its downfall more surely than any foreign enemy. Samuel Adams, the father of the American Revolution, said, "While the people are virtuous they cannot be subdued; but when once they lose their virtue they will be ready to surrender their liberties to the first external or internal invader."[81] He went on to say that the greatest security from enslavement in a country is virtue or morality among the people.

Everyone's fundamental rights are threatened by a lack of morality in the people. People of character will desire to observe the law and will not willfully take the life, liberty, property, or reputation of others – that is, that will not violate the Second Table of the Ten Commandments. Consequently, people will not live in fear of other citizens. In addition, less government will be required in a virtuous nation. Since fewer people will violate the law, a large police force and judicial system will not be needed. Law making bodies will also have less to do because prohibitive laws will be at a minimum, as citizens will constrain themselves.

In a virtuous nation the rulers will be moral. This produces more freedom because the rulers will not usurp individual rights through bad legislation and they will not steal from people through fiat money, excessive or graduated taxes, or other means. Consequently, people will not live in fear of civil government.

What is virtue or character? Virtue has been defined as a conformity to a standard of right, and also a voluntary obedience to truth. Character is a convictional belief that results in consistent behavior.

Character literally means "to stamp and engrave through pressure." This sums up nicely what God is doing in our lives. God's plan is to make each person like Him. Romans 8:29 tells us that God has predestined that we, as His children, are to be conformed into the image of Christ. He is building His character within us, or you might say He is stamping and engraving upon us

His image. He is doing this so that we might be examples of Him to the world and, also, that we may be able to fulfill His purpose for our lives.

A virtuous people is the basis of happiness in a society and is absolutely necessary for a state to long remain free. As human nature is corrupted, the foundations of freedom are easily destroyed.

Valuable characteristics of virtuous citizens include:

- They will have a concern for the common good above their own self-interest.
- They will vigorously participate in local, regional, and national government, and will seek to correct wrong conduct in public officials.
- If necessary, they will risk their lives, fortunes, and honor for their country.
- They will perform their duties and seek to have right conduct in public and private.

A free market economy is dependent upon the people being virtuous because such a people:

- Will not steal from their employees or others. Such theft increases the cost of goods and services for everyone.
- Will have a strong work ethic and be productive. This hard labor will cause the economy to grow.
- Will respect contracts.
- Will save and invest to acquire a greater return later.
- Will have a concern for their posterity and will seek to pass on a greater estate than they received.
- Will not waste public resources and will be good stewards of the environment.

Consequently, a lack of character in the people can produce the following: a stagnant or declining economy, corrupt laws, a lack of smooth transition from one political leader or party to another after elections, a corrupt military that may take control of the government, and increased power in civil government to attempt to solve the many problems that result from lack of character in the people.

A virtuous people will be vigilant to work to establish a free nation and then also to maintain it. Eternal vigilance is the price to maintain liberty. People of character will be eternally vigilant to secure their rights and demand that their government's power remain limited.

The founder of Pennsylvania, William Penn, explained the nature of civil government in the Preface to the *Frame of Government of Pennsylvania* (adopted April 25, 1682):

William Penn

> Governments like clocks, go from the motion men give them; and as governments are made and moved by men, so by them they are ruined too. Wherefore governments rather depend upon men, than men upon governments. Let men be good, and the government cannot be bad; if it will be ill, they will cure it. Some say, let us have good laws, and no matter for the men who execute them: but let them consider, that though good laws do well, good men do better: for good laws may want good men, and be abolished or evaded by ill men; but good men will never want good laws, not suffer ill ones.

It is true, good laws have some awe upon ill ministers, but that is where they have not power to escape or abolish them, and the people are generally wise and good: but a loose and depraved people love laws and an administration like themselves. That, therefore, which makes a good constitution, must keep it, viz: men of wisdom, and virtue, qualities, that because they descend not with worldly inheritances, must be carefully propagated by a virtuous education of youth.[82]

7. Faith in God and His Word

The foundation of the Hebrew Republic was belief in the true God and adherence to His righteous standards of living. A central intent of the laws He gave to Israel (and all mankind) was to keep them from idolatry, to keep them from serving and following false gods. We live in God's world, which was created to function in accordance with God's physical and moral laws. Violation of those laws brings trouble, while adherence to them brings life and blessing (Dt. 28; Lev. 26). God gave His Law to mankind in order to teach him how to love the one and only true God (Commandments 1-4), and how to love his fellow man (Commandments 5-10). In addition, obedience to His Word brings great blessings to mankind. Any nation desiring to be free, just, and blessed must adopt and obey His precepts.

The foundational principles (and, as we shall see, the framework) of a free society flow directly or indirectly out of the faith or religion of the people. The principles we have just examined all come from the Bible. Each one of these principles, which must be a part of people's lives for a free nation to be established and maintained, requires the indispensable support of the Creator.

With the principle of individuality, we saw that the uniqueness and value of man comes from his being created by God. Man becomes self-governing as he is subject to God and His truth. Morality cannot exist separate from religion. Man's most precious possession, his conscience, responds to right or wrong put in his heart by his Creator. The strongest force to bring union between a people is a common faith. Education that will propagate liberty must sow seeds of truth. All truth originates with God.

For the fundamental rights of man to be secure from government, the people must recognize that these rights are endowed by their Creator, and not granted by government. If people think that government, or man, is the source of rights then government can take them away. But if God gives rights to men, then they are inalienable.

To secure liberty for all men, the answer to the following question must be understood: "Who is the source of law in a society?" In reality, the source of law in a society is the god of that society. If man is the final source of the law, then the law will constantly change as man's ideas and understanding changes. God is the source of true law and His law is absolute. William Blackstone, the great English legal scholar, said that no human laws are of any validity, if contrary to the higher law of God.

The central goal of a Christian society is the worship of the true God. Laws and actions should encourage the worship of God and prohibit idolatry. God is our king as well as our savior, and His law is the scepter by which He rules. In studying the development of individual and civil liberty, it is readily apparent that the Christian faith has provided laws that have produced the greatest amount of freedom and prosperity in history.[83]

Christianity has produced the power or principles in the people necessary to support liberty. Certain aspects of this law of liberty are revealed to all men, in what Blackstone called the Laws of Nature. However, the primary way that God has revealed His law to man is through the Bible, the written word of God. To the degree that nations have applied the principles of the Bible, is the degree to which those nations have prospered and been free.

The great Christian statesmen of the Nineteenth Century, Daniel Webster, gave us this warning:

> If we and our posterity shall be true to the Christian religion, if we and they shall live always in the fear of God and shall respect His Commandments,... we may have the highest hopes of the future fortunes of our country;.... But if we and our posterity neglect religious instruction and authority, violate the rules of eternal justice, trifle with the injunctions of morality, and recklessly destroy the political constitution which holds us together, no man can tell how sudden a catastrophe may overwhelm us that shall bury all our glory in profound obscurity.[84]

Daniel Webster

Every nation is based upon some religion. Christianity brings, not only individual, but also civil liberty.

Chapter 8

The Government of Ancient Israel: a Model for Today

In a casual reading of the Pentateuch (or the Bible at large), or reading it as many people do today, looking merely for spiritual ideas, one would think little is said about government, especially regarding its form. Because of this pietistic perspective, many people think that the Bible does not present or endorse a specific form of government. Therefore to them, many different forms are acceptable. It is true there is no systematic presentation of a framework of government in the Bible, but it does provide much insight into what would be a good form, and it teaches many fundamental principles that should be incorporated into government.

God Himself gave birth to a nation. He established Israel with many specific details that we should apply to governments today. If He thought these components were good, it would be wise that we embrace them as well. In fact, studying the Law and the polity of ancient Israel reveal the great wisdom of God. His laws are the perfect standard of righteousness, justice, and equity. The form of government He established is the best model the world has seen.

What type of government did God establish for His nation Israel?

God started the nation of Israel and gave it principles of government. Under Joseph's leadership the Hebrews migrated into Egypt to survive a famine and ended up becoming slaves. Then God raised up a man named Moses, who was a Hebrew but grew up in the house of the Egyptian royal family, to liberate his people from slavery. After becoming a free people once again, God led Moses to organize their laws and form of government (Ex. 4:29; Ps. 107:32). The first representative republic on earth was established.

Prior to their deliverance, Israel had lived in slavery in Egypt for many generations. Therefore, when God delivered them out of Egypt and took them into the promised land, He was starting a new nation with a group of slaves, not the prime material for success. But over the

God used Moses to deliver Israel from Egypt and give birth to a new nation, one built upon the Law of God.

years this people — these slaves — became a great nation, so great that Israel was known throughout the world. The Queen of Sheba traveled to see Israel for she had heard of her greatness. Israel was beyond even what she had heard. How did this change occur? How did these slaves give birth to a nation that was free, just, prosperous, and virtuous (especially in comparison to the other nations)?

The first thing God did was to give Israel a set of laws. The overarching principles of these laws are contained in the Ten Commandments that God delivered to Moses on Mount Sinai. He obviously considered them important, because He wrote them with His own hand (Ex. 24:12; 31:18; 32:15-16; Ex. 34:1-4; 27-28; Dt. 10:1-4). God then expanded the principles in the Ten Commandments that Moses wrote down and gave to the people in what is called the Mosaic Law (see Exodus, Leviticus, Numbers, and Deuteronomy). This Law of Moses was the constitution for Israel. God required everyone to know and obey the constitution (Dt. 4:1-2, 5-14, 39-40; 5:1; Dt. 29:29; 1 Sam. 15:22), and give their consent to it (Ex. 19:5-8; Dt. 4). (When Israel later insisted on having a king, he was to govern with the consent of the people; see 1 Chron. 11:3 and section below.) Obedience to God's Law (His constitution) produces blessings (Dt. 28; Dt. 5:29; Ex. 19:5-6; Rom. 10:5). Thus, the rule of law (constitutionalism) is foundational for any government desiring to be free and desiring to follow God's blueprint for the best form of government.

The laws of Moses were unique in ancient history, quite different from the laws of Hammurabi of Babylon made about 200 years earlier. The Mosaic Law was much more humane, equitable, merciful, and respectful of rights, not just of male citizens but of all people including women, children, and slaves.

God did not invent the Ten Commandments just for the nation of Israel. They are actually a summary of the moral law of God that existed from the beginning of His Creation, and in fact, before Creation because they reflect the moral character of God Himself.

At creation, God gave to Adam (representative of all mankind) a law that He required him to obey. This moral law written in his conscience revealed how God's moral universe functioned. The law flowed from the nature and character of God Himself. God also gave Adam the capacity to obey it. Obedience brought him life, while disobedience brought death (see Genesis 1-2).

This law was still a perfect rule of righteousness even after the fall, although man in his fallen state could no longer clearly know and understand it. Therefore, God in His mercy, revealed the law in written form, as summarized in ten commandments and two tables, to His covenant nation of Israel (Matt. 22:37-40; Exod. 20:3-18). The books of the Law delivered by God to Moses for the people also contain various case laws (see Exodus, Leviticus, Numbers, Deuteronomy), which were specific applications of the general principles contained in the Ten Commandments (the moral laws of God).

In addition, God gave Israel ceremonial laws regarding means of worship and various ordinances that prefigured the work of Christ (see Lev. 5:1-6; 6:1-7, and similar passages; Heb. 10:1; Gal. 4:1-3 Col. 2:17; Heb. 9). Since Christ fulfilled the ceremonial law, they are no longer

God delivered His commandments to Moses but He also wrote them upon the conscience of all men.

applicable (Mark 7:18-19; Col. 2:17; Eph. 2:15-16). God also gave them certain judicial laws that set the physical nation of Israel apart as unique from all other nations (some people call these laws the holiness code). Since the New Covenant nation (made up of all regenerated believers) is not physical but spiritual, these laws are also not applicable for us today (although we can apply their principles in various ways).

The Decalogue provided for the protection of ten valuable "rights." A right is a just claim upon an express command of God, or in accordance with His will.[85] The following chart lists those God-given rights.

The Decalogue

Prohibited	Affirmed the Sanctity (or Right) of
1. Polytheism	God (sovereignty)
2. Idolatry	Worship
3. Profanity	Speech (vows)
4. Work on Sabbath	Time (rest)
5. Dishonor of Parents	Authority (family)
6. Murder	Life (individual)
7. Adultery	Love (contract)
8. Theft	Property
9. Perjury	Truth (reputation)
10. Coveting	Conscience

From the beginning God's purpose was not limited to Israel, but He desired that these laws and their blessings might be exported to all nations – nations who had perverted God's plan of civil government into pagan, centralized monarchy.

God gave Israel two things that none of the other nations had. He gave them His law and His presence. Deuteronomy 4:5-8 states:

"See, I have taught you statutes and judgments just as the Lord my God commanded me, that you should do thus in the land where you are entering to possess it. So keep and do them, for that is your wisdom and your understanding in the sight of the peoples who will hear all these statutes and say, 'Surely this great nation is a wise and understanding people.' For what great nation is there that has a god so near to it as is the Lord our God whenever we call on Him? Or what great nation is there that has statutes and judgments as righteous as this whole law which I am setting before you today?"

Great nations will have God's presence and God's law-word. This is what made Israel great and unique among all the nations. God's law was a template or blueprint to build a nation. It worked. Jesus said it is still a template (Matt. 5:17-19); it is for establishing and discipling a nation. Jesus said He came to fulfill the law, and that we must teach His law or we "shall be called least in the kingdom of heaven" (v. 19).

The Form of the Hebrew Republic

God not only gave Israel His Law, but He also directed the structure of their government and society in such a way that they could best learn and apply His law, secure God-given rights and liberties, and pass on biblical liberty to their posterity.

Israel was not a theocracy in the sense of God ruling the people from the top down. God ruled through His law and elected officials with the consent of the people. Biblical law empowers men to live free and happy, but so does biblical polity.

The framework of the polity of Israel is intended to serve as an example for those nations desiring to secure the proper purpose of government, which is the protection of the life, liberty, property, and happiness of the governed. The biblical form of government is also best for keeping the people from idolatry, in particular, from looking to government as their savior, provider, and source of rights. The belief that civil government or the state is the ultimate authority (statism) has been the greatest form of false worship in history.

Prior to the time of Moses, the Hebrews had a patriarchal form of government (as did most nations). Abraham, Isaac, and Jacob governed as independent princes with nearly unlimited authority. The twelve sons of Jacob exercised similar authority, but when their descendants multiplied, each tribe acknowledged a prince as its ruler (Numbers 1). This office was likely hereditary at first, but later became elective. Since the family formed the foundation of the nation, family government was primary. In fact, as the families of the descendants of Jacob multiplied, their leaders became the civil rulers and were called heads (Num. 17:3; 25:15; Jos. 22:14; 23:2) or elders (Ex. 3:16; 4:29). This was the case while they lived in Egypt. In forming the new nation of Israel, God incorporated their family-based leaders into a new framework of government.

The general components of the structure of Israel's government follow. The definitive work on the government of Israel was written by E.C. Wines in the early part of the nineteenth century. Much of the following is from his book, *Commentary on the Laws of the Ancient Hebrews, Book II, Organic Law of the Hebrew State.*[86]

Federalism and Local Governments

Israel was a federal republic where each tribe formed a separate state with their own government rulers. Each tribe had a voice in the national government through the senate and general assembly, and all were united under the common Mosaic Law. Every city had its elders, judges, officers, and rulers (Deut. 21:1 ff; Jud. 11:5-6, 11; Jud. 8:6, 14; Ruth 4:4, 9; Ezra 10:14; Deut. 16:18; Dt. 21:2), with the same diversity of governing officials as in the nation at large. Each family was represented in the Hebrew Republic.

Each tribe was a distinct and independent sovereignty, but worked in union with the other tribes for the common mission established by God in the Law. They were to provide for their own interests, but help the other tribes if necessary. No tribe had superiority over any other. Each raised their own armies and fought both independently and in union with other tribes. They levied war and made peace (see Jos. 17:15; Jud. 4:10; 1 Chron. 5:18-23).

Officers of Government

A group of officers, also called shoterim,[87] came into being among the Hebrews while they were in Egypt, but continued functioning after the Israelites came into the Promised Land. Moses told the people upon entering the land that they should appoint both judges and officers (shoterim) in every city (Dt. 16:18). The most important duty of the shoterim was "to keep the genealogical registers; to record accurately the marriages, births, and deaths among the people." Among a people where hereditary succession was primary, these officers performed an important function. Some of the shoterim would serve as representatives of the people in the senate and assembly.[88]

Chief Magistrate

Moses was the first chief magistrate of the nation, followed by Joshua. Judges served as the national executive for over four centuries until the people demanded a king. Though not what God wanted, He nonetheless allowed kings. None of these leaders had absolute power.

Moses established judges, who were more like our current governors rather than judges in courts. Judges were God's original plan for Israel's chief magistrate (2 Sam. 7:11). These judges were elected by the people; they served with the consent of the people. As the chief executive Moses was concerned about a successor to lead the people because he did not want them to be like sheep without a shepherd (Num. 27:15-17). At the instruction of God with the consent of the people, Moses chose Joshua to succeed him as the chief magistrate (Num. 27:18-23; Josh. 1:1-18). Judges assumed this role after Joshua.

The chief magistrate commanded the military in times of war and directed civil affairs in peace. Judges were not the supreme authority. God was the king over Israel, and He ruled through His law. Moses (and later judges and kings) was His viceroy, ruling under His law and in conjunction with the legislative assemblies (see next section).

Judges

A thorough study of the office of the Hebrew judges reveals:[89]
- The Hebrew judges held their office for life.
- The office was not hereditary.
- The chief magistrate was elected (for example, Joshua, Num. 28:19, 22; Jephthah, Jud. 11:4-11; and Samuel, 1 Sam. 7:5-8).
- They had authority in affairs of war and peace (see the example of Moses, Joshua, Deborah, and others), although not every judge led the armies.
- Their authority was limited and restrained by the Law and the other officials (Num. 27:21). They could not impose taxes on the people.

During the 450 years Israel had judges, the nation maintained their independence and prospered about 75% of the time. There were times of oppression and adversity, but this was only about one quarter of the years. Scripture presents these difficult times (see Judges), but of the peaceful and prosperous times little is written. For example the entire history of 120 years is presented by two brief statements: "The land had rest forty years" (Jud. 3:11), and "the land had rest for four score years" (Jud. 3:30). God's civil order produces peace, happiness, and blessing. Such extended times of blessings did not occur under the kings. In fact, the seeds of the destruction of Israel were planted when the people rejected God's form of government (and hence, they rejected God Himself), and embraced the pagan form of government.

Kings

Knowing the propensity of fallen, sinful man, God made a provision for Israel establishing kings. When they tired of being self-governed and fighting their own battles, the people demanded a king like all the other nations (1 Sam. 8). The Law has a provision for kings and limits their power:

> [14] When you enter the land which the Lord your God gives you, and possess it and live in it, and you say, "I will set a king over me like all the nations who are around me,"
> [15] you shall surely set a king over you whom the Lord your God chooses, one from among your countrymen [brothers] you shall set as king over yourselves; you may not put a foreigner over yourselves who is not your countryman [brother].
> [16] Moreover, he shall not multiply horses for himself, nor shall he cause the people to return to Egypt to multiply horses, since the Lord has said to you, "You shall never again return that way."
> [17] Neither shall he multiply wives for himself, lest his heart turn away; nor shall he greatly increase silver and gold for himself.
> [18] Now it shall come about when he sits on the throne of his kingdom, he shall write for himself a copy of this law on a scroll, in the presence of the Levitical priests.
> [19] And it shall be with him, and he shall read it all the days of his life, that he may learn to fear the Lord his God, by carefully observing all the words of this law and these statutes,
> [20] that his heart may not be lifted up above his countrymen and that he may not turn aside from the commandment, to the right or to the left; in order that he and his sons may continue long in his kingdom in the midst of Israel. (Deut. 17:14-20, NASV)

The biblical requirements of regal power include:

- God permitted kings (a constitutional monarchy) although this was not part of His original system of government for Israel. The people demanded a king (God allows people to receive the type of government their internal character can support). Reasons for their demand of a king include: lack of self-government, fear of being overcome by their enemies, the degeneracy of Samuel's sons, a lack of faith, longing for the pomp of royalty, and desire to be like all the other nations (1 Sam.

8). Thanks to God's foresight to give instruction regarding kings, the transition to royalty was accomplished in a peaceful manner.

- The people elected kings who God endorsed. The people via their representatives (the assembly) and the oracle of God must concur with anyone being elevated as king (Dt. 17:15). The first king, Saul, was chosen by God and confirmed by the people (see 1 Sam. 8-11). After Saul won the approval of the people, Samuel called a second general assembly (at a first gathering of leaders many opposed him as king) where Saul was approved as king. After his inauguration, Samuel resigned his office as judge. So God raised up judges and kings, but the people also confirmed/elected them. God anointed David for the throne (1 Sam. 16:13), and the people confirmed this choice. Judah first chose David (2 Sam. 2:1-4) while the eleven other tribes chose Ishbosheth, who served seven years, after which they freely chose David (2 Sam. 2:8, 11; 5:1-3). King Solomon was confirmed by the general assembly (1 Chron. 29:20-24).

- The king was to be a native Hebrew citizen (Dt. 17:15). Such a leader was more likely to know and obey the Law of God, which the Lord commanded (Dt. 17:19-20) and which was essential for the well-being of the nation.

- The king was not to multiply horses. Horses were used in offensive warfare. God did not want Israel to conquer other nations, but only to be involved in defensive warfare – to protect themselves from attack.

- Kings were forbidden to marry many wives. The leaders of surrounding nations typically kept a haram, seeking the most beautiful women of all nations to increase their pleasure. God forbid moral indolence, but He also sought to avoid the idolatrous influence of heathen beauties. Solomon's many wives turned his heart toward other gods.

- The king was not to amass great wealth; he was not to greatly multiply his silver and gold. Great wealth leads to a life of luxury which tends to corrupt. Hoarding of money by leaders also diminishes the circulation of money, which stifles the economy. (The same is true when governments spend a high percentage of the gross domestic product.)

- The king was to be a defender of true religion. He was to reign as a subject of God and represent Him and His justice. Kings had a hand in promoting public worship and reforming corruption in religion. King Josiah upon discovering the Law of God had it read to the people, which helped spark a return to true faith. Since the central theme of the Hebrew Constitution (the Law) was the worship of the One and only God, each component of government had some responsibilities toward this end. (Yet, there was a separation of the institutions of civil government and of religion – the church today. See Chapter 9 on the separation of jurisdictions.)

- The king was to rule in accordance with the Word of God, not his own will. The Law was supreme. God required the kings to read, copy, and keep the Law. They could not rule arbitrarily, but in accordance with God's wise and perfect precepts. They were not unlimited sovereigns, but constitutional monarchs. The limitations of the power of the kings were written (1 Sam. 10:25).

- The king was to be humble and gracious to his subjects. He was to see the people as his equals and as brothers. He was to honor the general assembly, the representatives of the people.

- Apparently, royalty was hereditary if the kings adhered to the above principles; otherwise, it was given to others by the concurrent will of God and the people. In every case, the people had to give their consent; hence, the position was elective. Kings would covenant with the Lord and with the people (see for example, Jehoiada, 2 Kings 11:17).

- Other powers of royalty include: Some kings served as commander-in-chief of the army, but this power was limited and the army in general was subject to the people. The kings were not the chief judge in the nation, as this separation of powers was important in preserving the liberty of the people. At times, kings exercised the right of pardon (David pardoned Absalom and a murderer, 2 Sam. 14:4-31.) While corrupt kings took land from citizens (1 Kings 21:15-16), this was contrary to God's command (Ex. 20:15).

Legislative Assemblies

1) Select Assembly or the Hebrew Senate

Israel had two different legislative bodies: a Select Assembly (Senate) and a General Assembly. The Senate was comprised of the princes, elders, or senators of Israel and represented the twelve tribes.

When Moses assembled a council of 70 elders to help him govern the people, he was continuing what had existed for some time. Israel had elders/leaders in Egypt (Ex. 3:16; 4:29). Along with these princes of the tribes, there were leaders of the families and clans (Ex. 6:14 ff), which, no doubt, formed a council of state or a kind of senate. Later on, under the Mosaic Law, the twelve princes of the tribes, plus 58 other leaders, made up a senate of 70 (Numbers 26). These leaders of pre-republic Israel had some sort of authority (Ex. 12:21, 28; Ex. 11:14), and it is likely the Israelites fled Egypt under their various banners since they must have departed in an orderly fashion. These 70 leaders were summoned to go up to the Lord (Ex. 24:1), and the Law shows that the council existed (Num. 10:1-4).

When Moses became overburdened with governing (after the Law was given, and hence under the new constitution), God instructed him to gather a council of 70 elders who would help bear the load of governing the people. Chosen from the tribes, this Senate was composed of respectable, able, and experienced men. They were solemnly inaugurated, anointed by God, and affirmed by the people (see Numbers 11). The senate performed a different role

"Moses Elects the Council of Seventy Elders," painted by the Dutch artist Jacob de Wit in 1736-1737, hangs in the Rijksstudio Museum in Amsterdam. This painting, which was commissioned for the interior of the City Hall in Amsterdam, the Netherlands, reminds us that Israel was a representative republic with elected civil leaders.

than the Jethronian judges (see below). It served as a permanent counsel to the chief executive. It was to uphold the Law and preserve peace. In addition to working for the well-being of the entire nation, it also represented the tribal interests since it was composed of leaders from all the tribes.

The senate was not the government, but only one part of it. Its decisions were to be submitted to the congregation (through the popular assembly) for its approval. The incident recorded in Judges 20 shows this dynamic. At times we see where the senate proposed an issue, the congregation decided it, and the king executed it (1 Chron. 13:1-3). The general assembly (Dt. 1:22-23) and chief executive (Dt. 1:13) took the initiative also. All three branches worked together, with checks and balances, to accomplish God's purposes for civil order and justice.

2) Popular or General Assembly

The General Assembly was at times called the congregation of Israel (Num. 10:2-4; Jud. 20). Numbers 10:1-4 shows there was an assembly of the whole people as well as a senate (the council of 70). When Moses blew one trumpet only the smaller leadership council gathered (heads of the thousands of Israel), while blowing two trumpets was for summoning the congregation (or rather their popular assembly).

The assembly was called by a number of different names: the congregation, the congregation of Israel, all the assembly, all the children of Israel, and the whole congregation of the Lord. Some people think this assembly referred to all freeman who had a vote on important affairs. Some think that at times every person voted himself, and at other times their deputies voted. Others think that only the authorized representatives of the people voted, both in the wilderness and in the land of Canaan.[90]

Both Moses and Joshua convened the whole congregation, but the logistics of this would seem to dictate that it was the people's representatives who gathered at these assembles. There were 600,000 men who would have been a part of these gatherings in the wilderness. Scripture says Moses spoke to the congregation, but Moses could not have possibly spoken loud enough to be heard by that number or even one-tenth of them. It is most likely he spoke to the leaders of the congregation as is mentioned in Numbers 1:16. In Numbers 16:2 these deputized representatives are called "leaders of the congregation, chosen in the assembly" (NASB). In Deuteronomy 29 Moses summoned "all Israel and said to them...." "All Israel" was "your chiefs, your tribes, your elders and your officers, even all the men of Israel, your little ones, your wives, and the alien who is within your camps" (Dt. 29:10-11). Moses could not possibly speak loud enough to be heard by the 2.5 – 3 million people. So it seems likely that the first named persons represented all of the men, women, and children. These leaders acted as the people's representatives. These assemblies of all Israel included "their elders and their heads and their judges and their officers" (Joshua 23:1; 24:1).

Functions of the assembly included:

1) Choosing rulers. The assembly affirmed God and His Law (Ex. 19); they affirmed Joshua to succeed Moses as chief executive (Num. 27); they affirmed Saul as king (1 Sam. 10:17-27), Solomon as king (1 Chron. 29:22-23), and Jeroboam as king (1 Ki. 12:20). There are many examples of the people choosing or affirming their leaders via the assembly that represented them.

2) Foreign affairs. The case of the Gibeonites is one example of the assembly being involved in foreign affairs (Joshua 9).

3) Civil authority. The assembly was involved in enacting a new law in response to the petition of daughters of Zelophedad regarding inheritance rights for women (Num. 27:1-9). The assembly had authority in criminal matters (see Num. 35:24-25; 1 Sam. 14:42 ff). They had some voice in ecclesiastical affairs as well (see 1 Chron. 13:2-4; 24:20-22).

Judiciary

Inferior courts

Upon first leaving Egypt, Moses judged disputes that arose among the people, but this quickly became a great burden. Following the godly advice of his father-in-law Jethro, Moses told the people to choose from among themselves rulers of thousands, hundreds, fifties, and tens, and he would appoint them over them to help judge (Dt. 1:9-15; Ex. 18:17-26). There were about 78,600 in all. This structure facilitated an important concept in the administration of justice: every person could have easy access to prompt and cheap trials. This principle was retained when they entered the Promised Land because God commanded them to appoint judges in all the towns according to their tribes (Dt. 16:18). The old English Saxons as well as King Alfred organized their leaders based upon this frame of government.

> **Form of the Government of Israel**
>
> Federal Republic – 12 tribal & local governments
>
> ❖ **Chief Magistrate – Judges and Kings**
> ❖ **Legislative Assemblies**
> ➤ **Select Assembly or Senate**
> ➤ **Popular or General Assembly**
> ❖ **Judiciary**
> ➤ **Inferior Courts**
> ➤ **Supreme Court**

Later on, the Levites generally filled this office of judge (1 Chron. 23:4; 26:29-32; 2 Chron. 19:8-11). Logically, they would make the best judges because they best understood the laws of the land as it was their duty to learn and teach them.

The character qualities of these judges are fitting for all leaders. They were to be "wise and discerning and experienced men" (Dt. 1:13), "able men who fear God, men of truth, those who hate dishonest gain" (Ex. 18:21). Three general qualifications for godly governing officials are: 1) Fear of God; 2) Christian character; 3) Biblical worldview.[91]

Supreme Court

The structure of the Jethroic judges allowed for appeals to higher tribunals, with Moses as the final appeal. This process of appeal existed in the land of Canaan as well (Dt. 17:8-9). The Levitical priests or judges served on this Supreme Court.

The chief function of the judges in Israel was to administer justice between man and man (Dt. 16:18). Some judges may have exercised legislative power as well, since Joshua summoned them to the legislative assemblies (Joshua 23:2; 24:1).

Like the chief magistrate and the general assembly, judges were elected in Israel. In examining both accounts of the Jethroic judges in Deuteronomy 1:9-15 and Exodus 18:17-26, the people chose their judges from among themselves, then Moses commissioned them to the office. This continued in Canaan as the people were to appoint judges is every town (Dt. 16:18). Even the supreme judge (Chief Magistrate) was chosen by the people. One example is that "the people made him [Jephthah] head and chief over them" (Jud. 11:11).

Oracle of God

The oracle of God – the Word of the Lord, written, spoken, and supernaturally demonstrated – was a vital part of the polity of Israel. The Hebrew Republic was founded upon Yahweh, the One and Only true God. The oracle of Jehovah was an essential part of the civil constitution. In fact, the original constitution was the Word of God spoken to Moses on Mount Sinai. Importantly, God asked that the people consent to Him and His Word as the supreme power of the state. Because of the acknowledgement of God as the supreme authority, some have referred to Israel as a theocracy. But it was not a nation governed directly by God from the top-down. Rather, it was governed by elected rulers under the Law of God, and for its success required each citizen to govern themselves in accordance with His Law from the inside-out.

The oracle (God's spoken revelation) was the source of the Decalogue (the Ten Commandments, the summary of the Mosaic code) and also the rest of the moral, political, civil, and religious laws. God delivered His law to the people by speaking it to Moses. He also wrote the Ten Commandments with His own finger, no doubt wanting to assure their accuracy and impress upon Moses and the Hebrews their importance.[92]

The word *oracle* is used numerous times in the Old Testament (KJV) and in every case but one denotes the most holy place in the temple (for example, 1 Ki. 6:5, 19-23; 8:6). One time it means the Word of God (2 Sam. 16:23). In the New Testament (KJV) it is used only in the plural, and always denotes the Word of God (Rom. 3:2; Heb. 5:12). The Scriptures are called "living oracles" because of their quickening power (Acts 7:38; Heb. 4:12).

The oracle – the revealed will of God – was also made known to Israel in the form of the cloudy pillar. By its movement, God showed them when He wanted them to journey and stop (Num. 9:17-18). God spoke to Joshua directing the military affairs of the nation in regards to the capture of Jericho (Joshua 6). The Hebrews sought the Word of the Lord many times regarding both civil and ecclesiastical law (see for example, Num. 4:6-10; 27:1-9; 15:32-36). The oracle came in a variety of ways: via leaders, prophets, an audible voice, a cloudy pillar, the urim and thummin, and written.

The Holy of Holies was called the *oracle* due to the nature of inquiry of the Word of the Lord. A man inquired "at the oracle of God" by means of the urim and thummim in the breastplate on the high priest's ephod as he stood in the Holy of Holies before the Mercy Seat (the place of God's presence), and God answered, most likely, in an audible voice (Num. 27:21; 1 Sam. 28:6). So the Word of God (the oracle) came as the priest stood in the most holy place. That this was done for the confirmation of Joshua as the chief executive indicates the people sought the Word of the Lord, and God answered, in matters concerning civil affairs.

God probably responded audibly because He had done so before. He spoke to Moses when he delivered the Law to him on Sinai (Ex. 20:1), but also Scripture says that Jehovah spoke to Moses many other laws (see Exodus). In particular, "when Moses went into the tent of meeting to speak with Him, he heard the voice speaking to him from above the mercy seat that was on the ark of the testimony, from between the two cherubim" (Num. 7:89).

From the above Scriptures, we learn that the oracle expressed itself in two ways:

1) By a voice from the shekinah. The shekinah appears to have been "a concentrated glowing brightness, a preternatural splendor," but not known if it was material or immaterial. It was expressed by the term glory. This is how the Ten Commandments and other laws were given to Moses (Ex. 20).

2) By consulting the urim and thummim via the high priest. The precise nature of the urim and thummim is not known. Scripture tells us that they were something put by Moses into the breast-plate of the high priest.[93]

The priests were often consulted on what was the oracle of the Lord. They often gave confirmation of God's Law. The oracle of God was sought by Israel to obtain wisdom in public affairs, not personal matters. The oracle was an extraordinary institution and was uniquely for Israel. It was a means of gaining divine wisdom for building God's covenant nation. However, it provides the example that all godly nations are to seek the Word of the Lord. In the New Testament era, we have the written oracle and the Holy Spirit to speak to us and give us wisdom. This godly wisdom is for all aspects of life. Some nations have sought the wisdom of God through the oracle of God (for example, Ireland under Patrick, Scotland during the Reformation, and the early American colonies), and as they applied His Word, they were greatly blessed.

The four departments of the national government – the chief executive, the legislatures, the judiciary, and the oracle of God – were to work in union to administer God's justice and advance His kingdom purposes. A good example of their collaboration is the enactment of a new law in response to the daughters of Zelophedad (Num. 27:1-9). Here there was agreement among the chief magistrate, the senate, the assembly, and the oracle of God.

The Levites and the prophets were two other very important components of the Hebrew Republic.

Levites

The Levites were one of the twelve tribes of Israel. God set them apart for His service, and in so doing called this tribe to fulfill the role of all the families of Israel, who were to consecrate their first-born males for the altar (Num. 8:16). Aaron and the subsequent priestly ministry were of the tribe of Levi. They performed ecclesiastical work, which not only included oversight of the temple and its sacrifices but also education, music, and social concerns. Many Levites also served in civil government.

The organization of the tribe of Levi helped it fulfill its unique godly purpose. Unlike all of the other tribes, the Levites received no landed property, but lived in towns dispersed throughout all of Israel. One primary function of the Levites was to learn, preserve, and teach the Law of God (Dt. 33:9-10). Since God's Law speaks to all of life, the Levites taught truth for all spheres of life: personal, ecclesiastical, political, economic, and civil. Living in cities located within the territory of each of the other tribes kept them close to the people, and hence, made it easier for them to fulfill their educational function. The Levites were to be experts in the law. As experts, they not only taught the people but also served as counselors to rulers. They were God's ministers of state.

The Levites had a national presence as well. The high priest, who served like a president of the tribe, had his residence at the capital of the nation. The priests and Levites were "to inspire a love of law and order; to promote peace; to cement the bonds of social and political union; to insure a constantly progressive civilization; in a word, to place continually before the eyes of all their countrymen that law, to which their own individual interest and happiness were indissolubly united."[94]

The church's mission today is to do what the Levites did in Israel. While Bible-believing churches fulfill their priestly function, most have neglected much of the other Levitical service. Education, social concerns, and especially political counseling have been largely neglected. Those called to the Levitical order today must fulfill its broad purpose if nations are to experience the spiritual, social, and political blessings God intends for mankind.

God chose the tribe of Levi and the priests (who came from the Levites) for the service of the temple. The priests and Levites were consecrated and affirmed by the people's representatives (Lev. 8:2-5; Num. 8:5-22; the assembly chose Zadok as the high priest, 1 Chron. 29:22). Hence, those individuals who were charged with religious, educational, and social affairs were accountable to the people through their representatives.

The Levites drew their livelihood from the other tribes. Consequently, their material well-being was directly linked to their fulfilling their mission to train everyone in the principles of God's Law because obedience to His precepts produced material as well as spiritual blessing. They were to teach all of the Law but also were to inspire the people to love it with all their heart, soul, mind, and strength. God organized the nation such that the self-interest of the Levites would promote that national interest. They would seek the peace and welfare of the cities, for in so doing their welfare would increase.

The Levites' income was affected by their failure: 1) If they didn't teach God's truth, the people would turn from God and not obey His command to give a tithe of his increase to the Levites. 2) The people would not be as productive without being taught character traits of industry, work, creativity, etc. 3) The nation would experience less peace and order, which could affect their productivity.

The Levites were subject to the provincial government under which they lived. Each tribe and locality had their own governments that worked in conjunction with the national government. Their teaching the common Law to all Israel was a primary means of bringing unity to the nation. The Law and Levitical education united the twelve independent tribes. Similarly, the Bible and education (via family, churches, schools and colleges) united the early American colonies.[95]

Knowledge is one avenue for obtaining power. To keep the Levites from becoming leaders of a tyrannical state, God had them subject to the provincial governments. In addition, they, like all the Israelites, were subject to the constitution of Moses (the Law of God). The Law was the master. It was greater than priests or kings. They were creatures of the Law. Similarly, God's Word is greater than the church or civil rulers today. Both the church and state have authority, but God's Word is superior to both of them, and both are subject to Him and His Law. The church and state are creatures of God's Word.

The Levites and priests had civil duties. They were political counselors, enlightening civil leaders about the Law. They also acted as judges. God via Moses declared that "every dispute and every assault shall be settled by them" ("the priests, the sons of Levi," Dt. 21:5). At least 6000 served in government in the time of David (1 Chron. 23:4; 26:29-32). The tabernacle, and the temple afterwards, primarily had a religious purpose, but it also had a political purpose. The people not only gathered there to worship, but to seek God for questions regarding public affairs. It was a place where the assembly of leaders gathered to hear the Word of the Lord.

Churches do not perform such a function today, but they did in early American history. They served as places for government meetings (for example, St. John's Church in Richmond was where the state legislature was meeting when Patrick Henry gave his famous "liberty or death" speech) and gatherings to discuss political affairs (for example, Old South Meeting House is where the Boston citizens met to decide how to respond to the landing of ships carrying unjustly taxed tea that England was trying to force the colonists to purchase.) Pastors, like the Levites, provided political education in early America via Election Sermons, Fast Day Sermons, Thanksgiving Day Sermons, and Special Anniversary Sermons, as well as via education in schools and colleges.[96]

The Levites' most important civil function was to educate the nation in biblical principles of life, personal and social, ecclesiastical and political. They were the literati of the nation. They were the ministers, educators, lawyers, professors, physicians, writers, historians, astronomers, and mathematicians. The arts and sciences were their domain. The possession and application of these spheres is necessary for the advancement of civilization. They were to train the people how to live in liberty, how to be obedient, free, and useful citizens. This is the mission of Christians, to advance the Kingdom of God. Christians must assume their Levitical function to fulfill their mission to restore all things (Acts 3:21; Is. 49:8).[97]

Under the New Covenant era those performing the Levitical function would include not only pastors, missionaries, worship leaders, and church workers but also teachers, professors, musicians, artists, and those involved in meeting social needs. If God's people performed these Levitical functions today there would be no need for government education and welfare, nor the taxes necessary to pay for these.

Prophets

The prophets were spiritual and political preachers and counselors. They performed both religious and social functions. Old Testament prophets are usually viewed as imparting spiritual truth, proclaiming divine decrees, and foretelling future events. They certainly were keepers of civic virtue and preachers of the kingdom of the Messiah, but they did much more. While not a direct component of the political system, they nonetheless had great influence in state affairs by speaking the truth to kings and leaders. They were counselors to the kings, sometimes by request and sometimes by God's unction. They were God's special messengers to the nation and its rulers.

The writings of the prophets are filled with political maxims (see for example Is. 47:7-14, which Samuel Coleridge says reveals the true philosophy of the French revolution of 1789[98]). Prophets often rebuked civil officials when they violated the constitution, that is, God's Law (for example, Isa. 1:21-24).

Scripture records in Deuteronomy 18:9-22 that God established the prophetical office. The Lord told Moses that He would raise up a prophet like Moses that everyone should listen to (v. 15). This passage certainly applies to Jesus, as Peter noted (Acts 3:22), but most scholars believe this also "contains the promise of a constant succession of inspired men, of which succession Christ himself was to be the greatest."[99] Biblical history indicates there was a line of divinely inspired prophets in Israel.

The passage in Deuteronomy 18 reveals something of the nature and purpose of the office of the prophet. God set up the office to give true insight into some future events. In contrast, false prophets inaccurately foretold the future. True prophets spoke in the name of the Lord, Jehovah, and their words were often about great judgment to come upon the rebellious people. At times the rulers claimed God's prophets were false prophets, but they had no grounds to convict them until they could prove falsehood. Jeremiah was tried for publicly foretelling of the destruction of Jerusalem, but he was acquitted in accordance with the law and precedence (see Jer. 26).

God called prophets from various tribes and conditions of life and used them as instruments of His justice. They spoke against corruption in leaders and the nation at large. For example, Nathan charged King David to be a murderer (2 Sam. 12:7), Isaiah rebuked the rebellious rulers (Is. 1:23), Ezekiel called the princes wolves (Ezek. 22:27), Zephaniah proclaimed the religious and civil rulers to be treacherous persons (Zeph. 3:3-4), and Malachi charged the whole nation with robbing God (Mal. 3:8).

The power of the prophet was kept in check by the great punishment to be inflicted upon anyone who prophesied falsely. They received the ultimate penalty of death, which was in part due to the great influence they had in the nation at large. They were not just speaking God's Word to individuals regarding their personal lives, but they spoke to rulers and the nation at large. Obedience or disobedience to their message affected the history of God's covenant people.

To insure this important office was filled with godly men, schools of the prophets were established. The purpose of these schools was to identify and train those whom God had called to counsel the nation. The schools trained men in piety and taught them a deep knowledge of the Mosaic Law. They prepared prophets to preach to the people, to counsel ecclesiastical and government leaders, and to reprove the nation of any disobedience. Ezekiel indicates that prophets served as watchmen for the nation (Ezek. 33).

In the New Testament era, the church is to fulfill the role of the prophet by speaking God's Word to the nations and its rulers. If the church (via those who serve as watchmen) does not warn the nation of its sin, God will hold the church (the watchmen) accountable. If the watchmen speak God's Word, then they are absolved from any consequences of the rebellion of those who sin (see Ezekiel 33). Just as many prophets of old failed in their duty, so the church has at times failed in its duty. The corresponding judgment affects the nation at large and the course of history. The watchmen have often fallen asleep, but when the watchmen have faithfully fulfilled their prophetic role, revival has come, the church has grown, nations have been liberated, and advancement has occurred in all spheres of life.[100]

In Summary

The scriptural truth presented above shows that a constitutional federal republic is the best form of government. It is the type of government God Himself established in His covenant nation. The more closely nations have copied this biblical government the more they have been blessed. The United States of America is a prime example.

There are great similarities in the governments of America and ancient Israel. Both were built upon a system of self-government and the rule of law. Both required all of the citizens to know and live in accordance with truth, which is why education in the

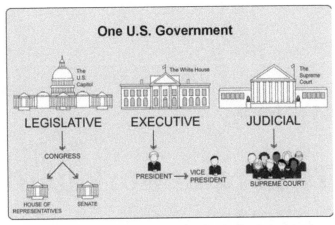

America's form of government is similar to ancient Israel's, with the three functions of government separated into three different branches.

Word of God was central, whether in homes, churches, or schools. They both embraced the biblical principles covered in the previous chapter as well as the framework of government presented in the next chapter. Both governments assume the equality of all men, and have as their primary purpose the protection of God-given rights and liberties. The Levitical function in Israel was carried out by the church in early America, teaching biblical truth in all spheres of life. The similarities continue in many ways.

E.C. Wines concludes that "the essential principles of our constitution are identical with those of a political system, which emanated from a superhuman wisdom, and was established by the authority of the supreme ruler of the world." Because of this, he goes on to write, "these principles are destined, in the good providence of God, to a universal triumph."[101]

The fruit of biblical government is liberty, prosperity, righteousness, justice, peace, happiness, and joy. In other words, it helps bring the Kingdom of God to earth (see Rom. 14:17). As God's kingdom advances in nations, their governments will embrace the power and form of a Christian constitutional republic. Such forms of government will follow the outpouring of the Spirit of God. Personal liberty comes first, but political liberty will follow if we copy God's great model of a constitutional republic.[102]

Chapter 9

The Framework of Biblical Government

Drawing upon the polity of the Hebrew Republic, the civil teachings of Jesus, and other Scriptural truths, we can represent a biblical framework of government with the following seven components.

1. Decentralization of Government

Jesus taught civil government should be limited in its authority. The tendency of pagan man is to centralize power, as witnessed by the building of the tower of Babel in Genesis 11. God condemned this man-centered humanistic public works project.

As discussed previously, the flow of power in a Christian society is from the internal to the external, from the bottom up, not the top down. Consequently, civil government should be kept as close to the people as possible. This can be accomplished by establishing a small national government and strong local and regional governments. The Hebrew Republic had a government that was a decentralized, family-based system. It had local town and tribal (regional) governments that were independent of the national government. The local officials, the elders of the cities, met in the gates (Ex. 24:1; Num. 11:16, 17).

Such a division of powers will be a safeguard against the tyranny of centralization since it will allow the people to most fully participate in government and to keep watch over the flow of power through the governing officials. For example, had Rehoboam listened to the people and his counselors, the nation of Israel may not have split (1 Kings 12:1-16).

History has shown that centralization of governmental power destroys the liberty and the rights of man. The way to have good and safe government is to divide the power among the people and the localities, instead of entrusting it to one body. Civil government in a country should be subdivided into many levels (local, regional, national). The power of each level should be clearly defined and sovereign in those defined areas. No level of government should be able to usurp the jurisdiction of another. A great majority of the power should rest on the local level.

The limited powers of the national government should be clearly defined in a constitution and involve those things which affect the country as a whole, such as defense, foreign policy, regulation of interregional and foreign commerce, citizenship laws, coining money, and copyrights. All other powers should remain with the people, or with the local, and regional governments. The powers of local and regional government can be written in a regional constitution and include such things as traffic regulations, business regulations, public works, voting procedures, and law and order.

Jesus Christ taught the principle of limited government and sphere sovereignty in Matthew 22:36-40. He said that "Caesar" may only do certain defined things, and that the other institutions, such as the church and the family, have their defined responsibilities and, therefore, sovereign rights of jurisdiction. This is true also between national and local governments. Author of the Declaration of Independence Thomas Jefferson said:

> The true theory of our Constitution is surely the wisest and best.... When all government...shall be drawn to Washington as the centre of all power, it will render powerless the checks provided of one government on another, and will become as...oppressive as the government from which we separated. What has destroyed the liberty and the rights of man in every government which has ever existed under the sun? The generalizing and concentrating all cares and powers into one body.... The way to have good and safe government is not to trust it all to one, but to divide it among the many.... It is by dividing and subdividing these republics, from the great national one down...that all will be done for the best.[103]

America's Founding Fathers understood the importance of decentralized government and limited national power, clearly seen in the United States Constitution. It enumerates eighteen powers of Congress (Article 1), a few powers of the president (Art. 2) and Supreme Court (Art. 3), and provides that all other power rests with the states and people (Amendments 9 and 10). How limited the power of Congress was in their mind is well expressed by James Madison, the chief architect of the Constitution, writing in 1792:

> If Congress can employ money indefinitely to the general welfare, and are the sole and supreme judges of the general welfare, they may take the care of religion into their own hands; they may appoint teachers in every state, county, and parish, and pay them out of their public treasury; they may take into their own hands the education of children, establishing in like manner schools throughout the Union; they may assume the provision for the poor; they may undertake the regulation of all roads other than post-roads.[104]

Obviously, modern civil leaders have abandoned this important idea as Congress has usurped the authority of the states, localities, and people. With that has come a loss of liberty.

2. Constitutionalism

The concept of constitutionalism began with the Hebrew Republic when Moses presented the Book of the Covenant to the people at Mount Sinai. It contained the Decalogue and the companion body of law. Contrary to the belief that some have of this being an arbitrary top-down imposition of law, the reality is that, although the laws were written by God, they were read and submitted to the people for adoption. The people had to agree to live by them before they would be of benefit (Exodus 19:5-8; 20:2-17; Dt. 17:14-20). This initiated the concept of a national covenant or constitution which must be agreed upon by the people before the government has legitimacy.

Later on, when Israel had a king, he had to enter into a covenant with the people where he promised to govern according to the Book of the Law, which was their constitution (1 Chron. 11:3; Deut. 17:14-20). For David, it mattered not that he was already anointed by a prophet of the Lord; he had to enter into a covenant with the people's representatives as well. This idea is articulated well in the United States Declaration of Independence which says that "just powers are derived from the consent of the governed."

This concept is part of the idea of federalism, a term which comes from the Latin word *foedus,* meaning covenant. In a decentralized government, a written constitution or contract will enable the people to be able to see if the national or regional governments overstep their authority. Any such usurpation of power can be resisted by the local and regional governments rallying together.

In a biblical government a constitution, and not the national ruling party, is supreme. The constitution should only be amended with the consent of the people and the local and regional governments.

A government of liberty will be a government of laws, not of rulers or of the majority. The law is supreme, not the rulers. Rulers are subject to the law as well as the people. Everyone is subject to the Highest Authority (Romans 13:1-7) and to the Law of God (Dt. 29:29; 1 Sam. 15:22; Matt. 4:4; Ps. 47). This provides a great security for all citizens. In a pure democracy, a simple majority (just over 50%) of the people rule. The rights of the minority could be in jeopardy under such a government. Therefore, the best form of democracy will be a constitutional democracy. Here, the law is supreme, and protects the rights of all people. (The term democracy is being used in the sense that power resides in the people, not that the people vote on every issue that arises in government because this is impractical. Since the people can most practically express their will on the local, state, and national levels through their representatives, the term constitutional republic is a better description. The term republic is associated with representative government.)

Throughout most of history people have been governed by laws imposed by their rulers. In this they had no choice. In a democracy the people will form their own constitution and consent to it. Hence, they establish a government of people's law, not of ruler's law. Both the people and the rulers are subject to the law. This is essential for protecting the individual's rights to life, liberty, and property. Citizens must not only be protected from harmful acts of other citizens, but also from abuses by their own government. Since the law is supreme and not the rulers, the people will be protected from ruler's tyranny.

A constitution will define and limit the power of government. It acts as a chain to bind down rulers from misusing power. Jefferson said, "In questions of power, then, let no more be heard of confidence in man, but bind him down from mischief by the chains of the Constitution."[105] To assure the constitution is not forgotten, it should be written.

A constitution formed by the people should not deny the rights of others. The laws will apply to all people equally, regardless of political position, religion, race, wealth, social status, or creed. Everyone is equal before the law in relation to protection of their life, liberty, and acquisition of property.

A parliamentary form of government is one in which the supreme source of law is the Parliament rather than a fixed higher written constitution. Parliament then tends to favor whatever groups gain the majority coalition and potentially may oppress the rights of minorities and individuals as it pleases. Any approach to rights based on ethnic or special group rights is ultimately dangerous to the rights of those groups or individuals out of favor with the government in power. Geographic representation is biblical, but ethnic or tribal representation is not (unless all of a tribe or ethnic group is within a specific geographical area and no one else lives there, Ex. 24:1, Num. 11:16-17).

A just constitution will be based on God's higher law – "the laws of nature and of nature's God." When Jefferson used this phrase in the Declaration of Independence it had a well-established meaning, described well by Andrew Young in an early civics textbook:

> The will of the Creator is the law of nature which men are bound to obey. But mankind in their present imperfect state are not capable of discovering in all cases what the law of nature requires; it has therefore pleased Divine Providence to reveal his will to mankind, to instruct them in their duties to himself and to each other. This will is revealed in the Holy Scriptures, and is called the law of revelation, or the Divine law."[106]

The laws of nature are the revelation of God in His creation and in man's conscience; the laws of nature's God are the revelation of God in the Bible. Biblical constitutions are built upon this Christian idea of law.

3. Separation of Powers

The Bible recognizes the three functions of all governments: legislative (makes the law), executive (carries out or executes the law), and judicial (judges violation of or interprets the law). Isaiah 33:22 says, "The Lord is our judge, the Lord is our lawgiver, the Lord is our king; He will save us." God being perfect and all wise can exercise all functions righteously, but sinful, finite men cannot. As discussed in the previous chapter, God separated these powers in the government of Israel as a safeguard against abuse.

A difficulty in forming any government where men are over men is that you must first enable the government to control the governed and then insure that the government controls itself. Men tend to abuse power, especially if they are given too much. It has been said that all power tends to corrupt; absolute power corrupts absolutely.[107] Due to this tendency of abuse, power must be limited in our civil rulers.

We have seen that prescribing specific powers in a constitution is one way to accomplish this. Another way is to separate governmental powers into different branches with different personnel running each branch. Every government (whether a monarchy, oligarchy, democracy, et cetera) exercises legislative, executive, and judicial functions. A division of functions and personnel between these three departments can be accomplished by setting up three separate branches with prescribed powers (in a constitution), where no person should serve in any two branches at the same time. This serves as an internal control of abuse of governmental power. Since men are not angels and tend to lack self-control, separation of powers will guard against tyranny.

The French political writer, Montesquieu, wrote in *The Spirit of Laws* (1748):

> When the legislative and executive powers are united in the same person, or in the same body of magistrates, there can be no liberty; because apprehensions may arise, lest the same monarch or senate should enact tyrannical laws, to execute them in a tyrannical manner. Again, there is no liberty, if the judiciary power be not separated from the legislative and executive. Were it joined with the legislative, the life and liberty of the subject would be exposed to arbitrary control; for the judge would be then the legislator. Were it joined to the executive power, the judge might behave with violence and oppression.[108]

Tyranny will result when legislative, executive, and judicial powers are all accumulated in the same hands, of one, a few, or many, regardless of how rulers come to office (whether hereditary, self-appointed, or even elected). Simply giving power to the people and allowing them to elect their leaders is not an assurance of securing liberty for all. One thousand despots would be as oppressive as one. We do not want to establish an elective despotism. Separating governmental powers into three branches is one of many controls on the government needed to keep the people's rights and liberties from being endangered.

The three branches should be independent of each other with no one branch having total control of another. As an example, the legislative branch should not be able to remove the executive or judiciary very easily; and the executive should not be able to dissolve the legislative or judiciary. While independent, these branches should not be completely separate, but should band together through a system of checks and balances. This will permit each branch to guard against one department encroaching into another, which would result in tyranny.

An example of checks and balances is the executive having the right to veto laws passed by the legislature, and the legislature being able to override the veto with a larger percentage vote by their members.

A well-defined system of checks and balances will help maintain the separation of powers in three branches. While a separation of powers will produce some conflict between the branches of government, this will assist in preserving the three branches of government and the system of checks and balances. To preserve them is as necessary as to institute them.

The various departments in the Hebrew Republic helped to balance power. The judge, senate, and assembly checked one another and all of these were checked by the Word of God. The role of the Levites and the prophets present examples of other ways God helped check potential abuse of power.

There are two sources of political and personal power: knowledge and property. God desired every family in Israel to possess both of these. In the Hebrew national structure, the Levites, having support via the tithe to study the law and truth, had access to great knowledge, but their potential for great power was checked in that they did not own lands. They did own houses in the cities where they lived. These cities were dispersed throughout the nation, which enabled them to more easily educate all the people, which was part of their mission. Their success empowered the people and advanced liberty. Their dispersion throughout the nation was also a check upon them easily forming any dangerous movements. The constitution of Israel enabled the Levites to perform their good and necessary function but also provided checks upon them from becoming too powerful. This is one of many wise provisions in the Hebrew law (constitution).

Bicameral Legislature

A bicameral national legislature is one where the responsibilities for making law is divided among two groups or "houses." One reason for dividing it is to create a check or safeguard, so that before a law goes into effect it must pass the vote of two houses, and then be approved by the chief executive. This structure is based upon the biblical view of man, who being sinful tends to abuse power.

In creating two houses in the legislature there should be a clear delegation of authority concerning which laws originate in each body. For example, one house could have the exclusive power to make laws dealing with taxing and spending and the second body could simply have the power to veto it. The second house could make laws dealing with war, defense, and foreign affairs, while the first house would have veto power over it.

In determining how the two houses are constituted, the Bible shows that it should be done in a way that one house represents regions or states and the other house represents individuals/families in a numerical population. As representatives of a region or state, the members of the first house ought to be chosen by the state or regional legislatures so that the interests of those areas as a whole would be best represented and deter centralization of power. State or regional legislatures will know how to best pick a representative who will be knowledgeable and qualified to work for their state's or region's concerns.

The other house, however, needs to be organized so that its representatives are elected by the people directly to speak on their behalf on various issues. It is this body, which is directly answerable to the people, that should be given the most power over the purse — the power to tax and spend.

The Hebrew Republic had a bicameral legislature (see Chapter 8). This model of government was incorporated by the United States of America in its original Constitution, with the Senate selected by the state legislatures and the House of Representatives elected directly by the people in districts determined by population. In 1913, however, an amendment to the Constitution made the Senate an elected body directly selected by popular vote, which was a step away from the biblical model.

4. Impartial Judiciary and Trial by Jury

Another check on sinful men abusing their governmental powers is having a court system with judges independent of the executive or legislative branch. In a nation under law, any violation of the law requires a judge. Wrongdoers must be punished and required to make restitution to deter crime, yet, there must be an orderly process of justice where the guilty and innocent are distinguished. Judges should not only be knowledgeable of the law, but also honest, refuse bribes, and not show favoritism.

The Hebrew Republic emphasized an independent and impartial judiciary (2 Chr. 19:5-10; Ex. 23:1-3; Deut. 17:6; Lev 20). Judges, like all officials, were to be men of Christian character, knowledgeable of the law, and possessing a fear of God (Ex. 18:21; Deut. 1:13), because justice requires good judges and leaders (Dt. 16:18-20). Bribery of judges was forbidden (Ex. 23:8; Dt. 16:18-20; 27:25; 1 Sam. 8:3).

All people had equal justice under the law, with swift and cheap trials by impartial judges. Many courts of various grades were established in every town (Dt. 16:18), with rulers over thousands, hundreds, fifties, and tens (Ex. 18:21). Hence, justice could be had by all men without going far, waiting too long, or paying too much. In addition to lower courts with many appeals, there was also a supreme court (Dt. 17:8-9).

God's law is just and protects the innocent. It assumes one is innocent until proven guilty, declares there is a right to due process of law, says a person cannot be forced to testify against himself, states that accusers must be personally present to confront those charged with a crime so they may be cross-examined, and establishes the right to appeal to a higher court. The Bible provides many safeguards for people charged with crimes.

Safeguards of those Accused of Crimes

- Scripture requires a formal accusation before a trial begins (Num. 35:12; Job 31:35).
- The right for accused to remain silent and not testify against himself (Num. 35:30; Deut. 17:6; 19:15; Mark 15:3-5; Mt. 27:14).
- The prosecution has to bring witnesses (Dt. 17:8-9).
- No torture to extract testimony; no coerced testimony.
- All trials are to be public; no secret trials (Deut. 16:18; 17:5).
- Testimony must be corroborated by 2 or 3 witnesses (Dt. 19:15-21; 17:6; Num. 35:30).
- Witnesses who give false testimony (perjury) are subject to the penalty attached to the crime under consideration (Dt. 19:18-21).
- Accused is innocent until proven guilty (Deut. 25:1-2; Is. 43:9; Dt. 17:6; Acts 23:3).
- The accused has the right to face his accusers and question them (Job 40:2; Psalm 50:21; Isa. 50:8).
- The right of self-defense (Deut. 1:16-17; 17:9; John 7:51)
- A right to a speedy trial (Ezra 7:26; Eccl. 8:11; Mt. 5:25)
- The witness is to take an oath before testifying (Ex. 22:10-11).

- A witness cannot refuse to testify at a criminal trial if called to do so (Lev. 5:1).
- At times a person has a right to a trial by jury (at least in some fashion) (Num. 35:12, 24-25; Josh. 20:6).
- Capital punishment is to be enforced impartially, and only after full and proper (swift) legal proceedings.
- Where execution is necessary it is to be public (Deut. 17:5, 13).
- Witnesses are to take part in the execution of convicted capital offenders (Deut. 17:7).
- Capital punishment is not to be enforced in a spirit of maliciousness or revenge (Matt. 5:38-44), but used only as God directs.

When these biblical safeguards are followed, the chance of the innocent being condemned is eliminated or reduced to near zero percent. The Bible gives more protection to both criminals and victims than America's present court system does, and much more than all other nations.

History is replete with examples of judges manipulated by government authorities to further their political agenda. An independent judiciary is essential to ensure that the written boundaries established by a constitution are maintained. The judicial system should be made up of individuals who will not be swayed by political pressures. (The Founders of America had the federal judges chosen by the people's representatives, rather than directly elected, as a means of separating them from potential political pressures. On the other hand, in many states the people elect their judges.) The courts are the ones who keep an eye on the legislative and executive branches of government and determine their faithfulness to constitutional standards (although they are not to be the final arbiter of what is lawful[109]).

Individual judges, even if un-elected, may at times be manipulated by government leaders or others to render unjust decisions against political opponents of the government. Therefore, in order to protect individual liberty, and guarantee a fair trial, there needs to be a judicial system that uses a jury drawn at random from society. These jury members should generally be on the same social level as the defendant. They also should be from the same city or geographical area as the defendant, yet should not know any facts about the case in advance that might color their perspective. The jury must be protected against government reprisals in order to be independent. A jury of peers should be effective because it can best make judgment about the defendant's character and the credibility of the witnesses.

Branch	Duties	Structure
Legislative (Art. 1)	1. Makes Laws 2. Appropriates money 3. Imposes taxes 4. Approves treaties and appointments	A Congress of two houses a. Senate – 2 members from each state b. House – number based on population (435 currently)
Executive (Art. 2)	1. Enforces laws 2. Makes appointments 3. Commands the Armed Forces 4. Has power of veto	a. A President b. A Vice-President c. Executive assistants appointed by the President (Cabinet and administrative agencies)
Judicial (Art. 3)	1. Interprets laws 2. Tries cases involving federal laws	a. The Supreme Court (9 members appointed by President and approved by Senate b. Lower federal courts (13 circuit, 94 district, 2 special)

The Constitutional duties and current structure of the three branches of the government of the United States.

There is freedom in a society that guarantees that neither life, liberty, nor property can be taken from the possessor until a dozen or so of his countrymen pass their sentence upon oath against him. Government becomes arbitrary without such a system of justice because the legislature could pass oppressive laws or a judge could deliberately misinterpret the law. Therefore, in addition to honest and knowledgeable judges, jury trials will protect the innocent and help uphold the law. To function best, citizens who comprise juries must possess Christian character and a biblical worldview.

The jury system was foreshadowed in the Hebrew Republic (Dt. 19:15-21) and in the teaching of Jesus concerning taking cases to the people (Matt 18:15-17). It was fully developed in British law over 1000 years ago. Governments, whether fascist or communist, have forbidden trial by jury. The United States, in contrast, conducts about 120,000 jury trials each year.

5. Civilian Control of Police and Military Forces

To protect citizens from criminals and enemies, both foreign and domestic, civil government wields the sword through military and police power. As a curb on the potential abuse of power by sinful men in government, the police and militia should be controlled and primarily constituted by civilians.

Peace, not war, was a central goal of Israel's government. In a time when war was the occupation of many nations, Moses set up a nation of peace. There was no provision for a standing army, rather all adult males comprised a citizen militia (Jud. 5:23), who, as landowners, preferred peace so that they would be able to cultivate their land. That all families owned land encouraged them to promote peace, as their livelihood and future depended upon it. A cavalry was also prohibited (Deut. 17:16). A cavalry is a chief aspect of offensive minded nations who seek conquest. The Bible teaches that a defensive war in a just cause is sinless.[110] Prohibiting horses for war also promoted political equality among the people because the wealthy could more easily amass a cavalry, making them more powerful.

Leaders should avoid war at all costs. The Bible says we should attempt to negotiate peace before fighting (Deut. 20:10). Jephthah did this (Jud. 11:12-27). Moses asked permission from other nations before marching through their land (Num. 20:14-21; 21:21-23).

In the Hebrew Republic the military was subject to the people. Firstly, the military was comprised of all adult men (the militia). Secondly, the militia divisions had their own locally elected officers (Dt. 20:9; Num. 31:14). Each of the tribes had their own militia. The members of the militia also supplied their own weapons which presupposed the right to bear arms (1 Sam 25:13; Num. 31:3; 32:20).

When national emergencies required the union of the tribal militias in a national army, the chief executive (judge or king) might lead the united army. In addition to the points above, the ability of the chief magistrate to form a professional army was checked by the people in that they affirmed or elected the judges and kings (see the previous chapter). Even though there was no provision under the Mosaic Law for a standing army, a small peacetime professional force of 600 men came to exist during the reign of King David. They served as his bodyguard and for use in emergencies until the militia could be gathered (1 Sam 23:13). The commanders of this force led the overall military strategy of the militia when they were called out in times of war, but the militia divisions with their own locally elected officers remained (Dt. 20:9; Num. 31:14).

Any attempt to prohibit the right of an individual to own arms is unbiblical and is a pagan attempt to centralize power (Judges 5:8; 1 Sam. 13:19-22). The leaders of the local militia could refuse to serve if they judged that a war that their nation was waging was unjust (2 Sam. 20:1; 1 Kings 12:16).

Military and police power is a necessity in society to protect citizens from criminals and enemies, both foreign and domestic. A wise and prudent people will always have a watchful and jealous eye over this power. The American statesman, Thomas Jefferson, said that "the supremacy of the civil over the military authority" is one of "the essential principles" of good government.[111] His draft of the Declaration of Independence condemned the British King for rendering "the Military independent of and superior to the Civil" authorities, and also for keeping "standing Armies without the consent of our legislature."[112]

Throughout the world today (as well as in the past) there are many armies that are supposedly the "people's" (that is, there to protect the people's interests as a whole) that are in reality being used by powerful government leaders to further their goals. Many nations experience military coups regularly and the generals of the armies run the nation rather than political leaders.

In order to ensure civilian control of the military, a constitution could establish an elected head of state ("president") as the commander-in-chief of the armed forces in war time. However, rules for the military should be established by elected representatives of the people other than the head of state. These elected representatives should not be able to spend money for armies for more than the period of time until they face re-election. This keeps the support of the military power by the representatives subject to the approval of the people.

The officers of the armies should not be appointed by the head-of-state, but by elected representatives from their own geographical area. The majority of a nation's army should simply be working citizens who have their own weapons and can be called together quickly. By doing this, no permanent army can exist that can be taken control of by a political leader. This system allows any citizen to own his own weapon, which will give everyone the ability to defend himself, and will also give a geographic area of people the ability to defend themselves from armies that do become pawns of the government.

The police force should be locally and regionally controlled and completely separate from military power. The head of the police forces should be elected and governed by local government. The rest of the police should be hired by the government as normal employment.

6. Election of Representatives

Another crucial component of the framework of free and godly nations is the election of representatives. As presented above, the governments of biblical nations will limit and check the powers of officials. They will also hold their leaders accountable through frequent and fair elections.

We saw in the last chapter how the government leaders of the Hebrew Republic were elected or confirmed by the general populace, either directly or through the people's representatives. This applied to all three branches of government – the chief executive, the assembly, and the judges. A few examples of Israel choosing their leaders include:

- People chose God as their king and consented to live under His Law (Ex. 19:8).
- People chose their judges as Jethro suggested (Dt. 1: 13; Ex. 18:21).
- People chose men from each tribe when Joshua was dividing the land (Jos. 18:4).
- People chose Jephthah as their chief magistrate or judge (Jud. 11:11).
- People chose the kings in Israel; for example, David (2 Sam. 2:4; 5:1-3).

Public officials are to be accountable to the people. They are to serve the people and not misuse their power. Samuel resigned his authority to the people's representatives and asked that he be held accountable if he had oppressed, defrauded, or wronged anyone (1 Sam. 12:1-5). When Saul was chosen king, Samuel wrote a document that limited the powers of the executive, which served as a restriction on future kings as well (1 Sam. 10:25; 2 Sam. 5:3; 1 Kings 12:4; 2 Kings 11:17).

Rulers should be elected by those that are ruled. Civil authority should emanate from the citizens. This is because governments are instituted to protect the life, liberty, and property of people. Government exists for the benefit of the people. It is to help the people obtain and preserve that which God says belongs to them. The Israelites did not directly elect every governing official.

Some were appointed by their representatives, but all were accountable to the people and to God's Law.

Frequent elections are essential; moreover, it is vital that elections be free. This means that those who run for office can do so without restriction of being from one party. One party may possibly dominate elections but it must come through winning the battle in the free marketplace of ideas. The right of any citizen to form a party and offer candidates for election is essential.

The vote in a nation must not be compulsory if it is to be free. It must be voluntary, plus it must be available to all citizens equally, regardless of race, color, or social status. To avoid potential pressure or reprisal, a secret ballot may be wise; although, public voting by all citizens gathered together in local communities would prohibit fraudulent voting.

Once the election determines the winner there must be a commitment to the peaceful transition and relinquishing of power by the previous office-holders. It is essential also that all competing candidates and parties work to be unified for the common good of the nation.

Another safety necessary to prevent majority tyranny and ensure more healthy gradual change in a nation would be to have staggered elections, where, for example, only a portion of the assembly be elected at the same time. Among other benefits, this would prevent radical changes from taking place without time for the electorate to fully weigh the potential consequences.

Those elected to office should meet the biblical qualifications given in Exodus 18 and Deuteronomy 1. Scripture says when the righteous rule the people rejoice. The electorate must be wise to choose such leaders. (See Chapter 10, section on "Biblical Qualifications for Governing Officials.")

7. Separation of Jurisdictions

The Bible teaches that civil government is one of three divine institutions — the family and church being the other two. Each institution is sovereign in its God-given sphere of authority. As such, civil government should not usurp the authority or responsibilities that God has given to individuals, the family, and church. Their jurisdictions should be kept separated.

Israel kept the government out of the areas properly under the jurisdiction of the individual, the family and the "church." Religion, the economy, the marketplace, the press, and the schools were not controlled by the state. The priests and the Levites were the "clergy" and the judges and assemblies of Israel were civil rulers. The "prophets" were primarily social reformers and statesmen among the people and included both clergy and non-clergy in their ranks. Separation of church and state, then, did not prohibit priests and Levites from holding public office or influencing politics as private citizens (Deut. 17:8-13; 2 Chron. 19:8, 11).

In biblical nations, the economy, press, church, and education would be separate from civil government control. Government must be constrained from claiming sovereignty over these spheres. The government may have a limited role in some of these areas; for example, they should assure that the marketplace is free and fair, by upholding contracts, maintaining just weights and measures, and implementing policies and taxes that encourage and support private property, individual enterprise, and a free market. Their role would be limited to protecting those who obey the law and punishing law-breakers.

The family is the foundational institution of mankind. God instituted it at creation. Its sacredness and preservation is of such importance that three of the Ten Commandments protect the family (Commandments 5, 7, 10). As the family goes in a nation, so goes the nation. If the family is weak, the nation will be weak. If the family reflects God's order and executes God's purposes, the nation at large will be strong, free, and prosperous.

Civil government should not undermine the family nor usurp any of its responsibilities, which includes providing health, education, and welfare. Likewise, civil government should not usurp the responsibilities of the church or of individuals. These various jurisdictions should be kept separate. Usurpation by civil government leads to loss of liberty and prosperity.

We should remember that the purpose of civil government is to protect law abiding citizens and punish criminals. It has no jurisdiction over the mind and the soul. Therefore, government should be prohibited from interfering with the church, the press, the school, and the marketplace. The American Constitution did this with the First Amendment: "Congress shall make no law respecting an establishment of religion, or prohibiting the free exercise thereof; or abridging the freedom of speech, or of the press."

———

A nation's religion determines the power and form of its government. The power (internal principles) necessary to produce a free republic originates in biblical Christianity (see Chapter 7); likewise with the form or framework of free governments. In *The Spirit of Laws*, French political philosopher Baron De

Montesquieu presented the idea that a nation's form of civil government is directly determined by its religion. Under the section on "Of Laws in Relation to Religion Considered in Itself, and in its Doctrines," he writes:

> The Christian religion, which ordains that men should love each other, would, without doubt, have every nation blest with the best civil, the best political laws; because these, next to this religion, are the greatest good that men can give and receive.[113]

He goes on to make the points, under titled sections: 1) "That a moderate Government is most agreeable to the Christian Religion, and a despotic Government to the Mahommedan" and 2) "That the Catholic Religion is most agreeable to a Monarchy, and the Protestant to a Republic."[114]

The seven components presented in this chapter comprise the framework of a Christian Republic. Derived from biblical ideas and Hebrew polity, this form of government will provide safeguards for the protection of individuals' God-given rights to life, liberty, and property. Though it is important to establish these biblical structures of government, it is more important for the citizens of a nation to continually work to place godly men in office who can establish justice even without an ideal form of government. It must be remembered, as William Penn wrote in his Frame of Government for Pennsylvania in 1682, "that though good laws do well, good men do better."[115]

Most importantly of all, to establish and maintain a government with a biblical framework, the people must have Christian character and a biblical worldview — they must adopt and obey the principles presented in Chapter 7. They must know how to live in liberty. They must be liberty men.

Chapter 10

Biblical Civil Duties

Government cannot perform its biblical function if Christians are not performing their biblical civil duties. God did not ordain civil government and then tell His people to stay out of it. Christians must be involved in government to be obedient to the Bible's commands. God's covenant people have biblical duties regarding government and civil affairs.

Christians who retreat from civil affairs are by their action agreeing with the devil's view of God's sovereignty; that is, God does not have legitimate authority over His creation and, consequently, man does not have legitimate rule over the earth as God's delegated vice-regent. However, as we have previously explained, God is Creator, Lord, and Sovereign, and governs all of His creation in His Providence. He created man in His image and commissioned him to rule over the earth. Satan rebelled against God as the absolute sovereign over His creation, thinking he had the right to govern on his own. Satan deceived Adam and Eve to follow him in determining their own reality and governing in their own authority (see Gen. 2-3). Even so, the commission to rule the earth under His Lordship and Law remained. God's covenant nation of Israel became a beachhead God used to re-establish His rule through His people. Christ Jesus made possible the restoration of His kingdom in the earth.

Man, being created in the image of God the King, was made to rule with Him over the earth. Jesus restored to mankind their position as sons of the King and as kings themselves (Rev. 1:6), and as such the redeemed are to be kings ruling over the earth in accordance with His Word and example. Hence, Christians must be involved in government, and they must fulfill their civil duties.

Individuals' Duties toward Government

From all the Scriptures and ideas covered previously, we can conclude our duties include at least the following:

1. Pray for civil leaders (1 Tim. 2:1-2)

We clearly have a responsibility to pray "for kings and all who are in authority," as a means to help bring about "a tranquil and quiet life" (1 Tim. 2:1-2). We are to pray for godly rulers, but also for wicked rulers. We can pray for God's protection and wisdom, but we may also need to pray for God to change a ruler's heart and override his action. "The king's heart is in the hand of the Lord, as the rivers of water. He turns it wherever He wishes" (Prov. 21:1, combining KJV and NASB).

There are many passages of Scripture that are directed toward rulers that can be useful as we pray for them. Using various Scriptures presented in this book will provide a great biblical guideline for praying for those in authority. There are a number of prayer ministries who offer prayer guides for civil leaders.[116]

2. Respect and submit to civil magistrates as God's ministers; obey all laws not contrary to direct biblical mandates (Rom. 13:1; 1 Pet. 2:13-14; Tit. 3:1)

God ordained civil government for the good of mankind. Government is our friend when it fulfills its biblical functions. It is God's instrument to protect law-abiding citizens and punish law-breakers. It is supposed to be a minister of God's justice. As such, we should respect government leaders and obey the civil laws of our nation.

However, obedience to government leaders does not mean unlimited submission, because we must obey God rather than man (Acts 5:29). While we should generally obey the civil laws issued by government, we have a duty to resist unbiblical rulers (although, this must be done in a biblical fashion, see Chapter 5). This includes removing bad rulers via voting and other lawful means. It also includes educating citizens in a biblical worldview.

3. Support and render appropriate service to government (Rom. 13:6-7, 17; 1 Pet. 2:13-14)

Appropriate service includes honoring leaders, performing military service, and paying taxes. Jesus said we are to give to Caesar the things that belong to Caesar, which includes paying taxes so that government can perform its duty (Mark 12:17). Jesus paid taxes, even those that were apparently not appropriate (Matt. 17:24-27).

Taxation

Civil government needs money to accomplish its responsibilities of providing defense, punishing evildoers, and keeping the peace. Gary DeMar writes:

> In the United States the Constitution is our "Caesar." We are bound to pay what it stipulates is our due. But, neither citizens nor civil representatives must assume that Jesus gave rulers a blank check in the area of taxation....Paul informs citizens to pay taxes due to civil authorities (Romans 13:7). Notice that Paul does not say "What they want." The state must limit taxing authority to those areas specified by God's word.[117]

Most current taxes are unbiblical and hence unjust. A progressive income tax is a non-biblical means of taxation that destroys personal property rights. This and other oppressive forms of taxation have come upon our nation as we have refused to govern and provide for ourselves as God intended us to. When Israel tired of being self-governed and asked for a king to rule over them, they got a king with greater centralization of power. One consequence of this was the confiscation of their property through taxes (see 1 Samuel 8).

Some current taxes that are unbiblical include:

1. Income tax (especially graduated income taxes) — God requires men to give to Him a tithe (10%) of their increase. Among other things, this is a recognition of His ownership of all things. It is a way to show tribute to the Lord. Allowing government to tax ones income is, in essence, acknowledging government's ownership of all things. To give civil government more than God requires would indicate giving of a greater allegiance, which is idolatry.

2. Property tax — "Civil government in the United States, in direct violation of biblical law, owns all the land in the country, and rents some of it to its citizens. If you do not pay the property tax (rent), you will be evicted.

This is theft. The government has no right whatsoever to tax property, and the principle of eminent domain is a claim to deity. It is specifically forbidden in Scripture (I Sam. 8:14; I Kings 21; Ezek. 46:18)."[118]

3. Inheritance taxes — In a Christian economy the children will be wealthier than their parents because the estate will continue to grow and be built up with each generation. This is one way the kingdom of God advances over time. Inheritance taxes thwart this. Such taxes take the fruit of a man's labor after he dies and before his children receive it, which is nowhere allowed in the Bible. Godly children should not have to start at the bottom when they begin their life and calling. Inheritance taxes diminish the wealth and effectiveness of each generation to contribute to the increase of His kingdom in the earth.

The Bible mentions two kinds of taxes that were used in the Hebrew Republic:

1. Head Tax or Poll Tax (Ex. 30:11-16) — This tax supported the state in its duties. It was a uniform tax that each male over age 20 paid. It was of necessity small so the poor would not be oppressed in paying it. Each man's life has equal value and needs equal protection; hence, each man should pay equally for that protection.

2. Tithe — A tenth of each person's increase was given to the priests and Levites for them to meet the necessary ecclesiastical and social functions of society. It supports the church and aspects of welfare, education, and other godly social needs. We could say the tithe is a "tax" on people's income (on their increase), although it is voluntary and not given to civil government. If citizens would tithe, the amount of money the civil government would need to collect would be drastically less.[119]

To move from our present tax system to a biblical tax system will require great character and understanding that will only come via true revival. Biblical gradualism would likely require interim steps along the way. So in conjunction with less and less government spending, we might replace graduated income taxes with a national sales tax (or a flat income tax). With continued decline of government spending (accompanied by individuals increasingly fulfilling their duties to provide education, health, and welfare, and by tithing so as to provide many social needs, along with the private sector meeting many needs) a small head tax could support a very small civil government. This state of great liberty is only possible if biblical transformation takes place in the nation.

4. Educate yourself and others about biblical government and civil duties; raise up godly leaders via biblical education — Perform Levitical Function

When Israel instituted a new form of government (monarchy), Samuel taught them about it and wrote it in a book (1 Sam. 10:25). He educated them in politics. Jehoiada the priest taught King Jehoash (2 Kings 12:2). Jehoash was raised in the House of the Lord, being educated by the priest, and as a consequence he did what was right (2 Kings 11:21, 3; 2 Kings 12:2). Since all Christians are priests before the Lord, we should all perform this educational Levitical function; however, this is especially true for pastors, teachers, and church leaders. Church leaders should teach their parishioners what the Bible says about government, as well as help equip those people who God calls to civil service.

Free nations are dependent upon the church teaching biblical principles of liberty and government. Noah Webster wrote:

Noah Webster

> In my view, the Christian religion is the most important and one of the first things in which all children, under a free government, ought to be instructed.... No truth is more evident to my mind than that the Christian religion must be the basis of any government intended to secure the rights and privileges of a free people.[120]

Clergy in early America performed this vital function, and consequently discipled the nation in fulfillment of Jesus' Great Commission (Matt. 28:18-20). Rev. John Witherspoon is an excellent example. Witherspoon moved from Scotland to America in 1768 to become president of the College of New Jersey (Princeton). He was elected to Congress, signed the Declaration of Independence, and served on over 100 committees during America's struggle for independence. He is said to have had more influence on the monetary policies found in the Constitution than any other man.

Rev. John Witherspoon trained the men who gave birth to the nation.

Through his role as an educator, John Witherspoon shaped the men who shaped America. During his tenure as president of the College of New Jersey, there were 478 graduates of what became Princeton University. Of these, at least 86 became active in civil government and included: one president (James Madison), one vice-president (Aaron Burr), 10 cabinet officers, 21 senators, 39 congressmen, 12 governors, a Supreme Court justice (Brockholst Livingston), and one attorney general of the United States (William Bradford). Nearly one-fifth of the signers of the Declaration of Independence, one-sixth of the delegates of the Constitutional Convention, and one-fifth of the first Congress under the Constitution were graduates of the College of New Jersey.[121]

The following is an excerpt from a sermon entitled "The Dominion of Providence over the Passions of Men" that Witherspoon preached on May 17, 1776, in observance of a Day of Fasting and Prayer called for by Congress:

> Upon the whole, I beseech you to make a wise improvement of the present threatening aspect of public affairs, and to remember that your duty to God, to your country, to your families, and to yourselves, is the same. True religion is nothing else but an inward temper and outward conduct suited to your state and circumstance in providence at any time. And as peace with God and conformity to him, adds to the sweetness of created comforts while we possess them, so in times of difficulty and trial, it is in the man of piety and inward principle, that we may expect to find the uncorrupted patriot, the useful citizen, and the invincible soldier. God grant that in America true religion and civil liberty may be inseparable, and the unjust attempts to destroy the one, may in the issue tend to the support and establishment of both.[122]

The history of America shows that biblical education is central to the advancement of liberty and prosperity in history. J. Wingate Thorton summarized the role of the clergy in the birth of our nation writing, "To the pulpit, the Puritan pulpit, we owe the moral force which won our independence."[123] Such a significant role did not begin at the time of the

American Revolution, but it was one that the church and her ministers had played from the beginning of the colonies.

Ministers were the primary educators in early America.

As the primary educators of the colonial period, the clergy had a tremendous impact upon the character and thinking of the people. Professor Harry S. Stout of Yale University writes: "The average weekly churchgoer in New England (and there were far more churchgoers than church members) listened to something like seven thousand sermons in a lifetime, totaling somewhere around fifteen thousand hours of concentrated listening." These statistics become even more significant when one considers there were essentially no "competing public speakers offering alternative messages. For all intents and purposes, the sermon was the only regular voice of authority."[124]

Ministers were the primary educators not only at churches but also at schools, academies, and colleges. Many of the Founding Fathers were tutored by ministers, including Thomas Jefferson, James Madison, George Mason, Patrick Henry, and Noah Webster. Those who attended college would have been trained by ministers as well. Through their biblical teaching, pastors guided the American people through their struggle for independence and freedom.

Rev. George Duffield was pastor of Pine Street Presbyterian Church from 1772 to 1790. He served as chaplain of the Continental Congress and of the Pennsylvania militia during the war. Duffield delivered many fiery, patriotic sermons to the many prominent men who attended his church. He inspired many to action, including John Adams, who was a member of his congregation while in Philadelphia.

In May 1776 John Adams listened to a sermon of Rev. Duffield that likened the way King George III treated the Americans to the way Pharaoh had treated the Israelites. Duffield concluded that God intended for the Americans to be liberated just as He intended the Israelites to be liberated. On May 17 Adams wrote to his wife:

MORAL VIEW OF RAIL ROADS.

A

DISCOURSE,

DELIVERED ON

SABBATH MORNING, FEBRUARY 23, 1851

Sermons were often printed and distributed widely. They addressed every area of life, like this one on "Moral View of Railroads."

Is it not a Saying of Moses, who am I, that I should go in and out before this great People? When I consider the great Events which are passed, and those greater which are rapidly advancing, and that I may have been instrumental in touching some Springs, and turning some small Wheels, which have had and will have such Effects, I feel an Awe upon my Mind, which is not easily described. G[reat] B[ritain] has at last driven America, to the last Step, a compleat Seperation from her, a total, absolute Independence.[125]

J.T. Headley writes of the influence of Rev. Duffield:

The patriots of the first Congress flocked to his church, and John Adams and his compeers were often his hearers.... In a discourse delivered before several companies of the Pennsylvania militia and members of Congress, four months before the Declaration of Independence, he took bold and decided ground in favor of that step, and pleaded his cause with sublime eloquence, which afterwards made him so obnoxious to the British that they placed a reward of fifty pounds for his capture.[126]

Later on in that sermon, Duffield delivered a prophetic word we must heed today: "Whilst sun and moon endure, America shall remain a city of refuge for the whole earth, until she herself shall play the tyrant, forget her destiny, disgrace her freedom, and provoke her God."[127]

We previously examined how Rev. John Witherspoon discipled the nation by training many of the Founding Fathers. If the pulpit had only given

Witherspoon to the Revolution it would deserve everlasting remembrance. But the pulpit gave much more: ministers taught the nation. They performed their Levitical function. The clergy took the task of teaching all the truth of the Scriptures seriously.

In addition to sound theology and personal matters of faith, their sermons addressed all areas of life. A few sermon topics from the founding era include: education, marriage, ardent spirits, the poor, social justice, old age, sodomy, gambling, comets, earthquakes, soldiers and patriotism, artillery, fire, Stamp Act repeal, Thanksgiving Days, civil government, bridge building, eclipses, "Moral Uses of the Sea," discovery of a new planet, railroads, medicine, snow and vapor, property, election sermons, and execution sermons.

They also educated the nation through their books and writings. Moral and religious catechisms were common for use in the church and school. Rev. John Wise wrote "The Law of Nature in Government" in 1717 which was so influential that it was reprinted in 1772 and studied by the civil leaders. Sections of this work appear word for word in the Declaration of Independence. When Thomas Paine wrote his anti-Christian work, *Age of Reason*, ministers strongly responded, including Bishop R. Watson's excellent defense of the faith, *An Apology for the Bible*.

Ministers wrote influential history books, such as *The Great Works of Christ in America* by Cotton Mather and *A General History of the World* by Frederick Butler, educational books, such as Rev. William Holmes McGuffey's series of *Readers*, and many others. In addition, ministers started many schools and colleges, serving as professors and presidents, they were the primary newsmen, and they wrote laws, constitutions, and other civil documents. These and other factors led Alice Baldwin to write that "the Constitutional Convention and the written Constitution were the children of the pulpit."[128]

The church and its leaders—those performing the function of the Levites—were instrumental in the birth of America, the land of liberty. This had been true in the advancement of liberty throughout the Christian era.[129] While most pulpits in America and the nations have neglected this duty in recent times, there are many Christian leaders who are working to disciple the nations. The Providence Foundation (led and co-founded by the author) is one of those organizations that God has used to educate and mobilize others for service in the public square. (See our website for many reports of impacting America and the nations: providencefoundation.com)

DIVISIONS OF HISTORY.

A. The history of the creation, as recorded by Moses in the first chapter of Genesis ; comprising the formation of all those vast and luminous worlds that fill the unbounded extent of heaven with their majesty and splendor, the sun, the earth, the moon and stars innumerable ; the creation of animate nature, with man for its head, the covenant between man and his God ; man's violation of that covenant which brought death into the world and all our woe ; the early promise to man that the seed of the woman should bruise the serpent's head, and that man should be restored to the lost favour of his God.

Q. What do we know of God, and his character?

A. The character of God is best explained and understood by his works of nature and volume of Revelation. God is known to us by his attributes, and he may have many others beyond our comprehension. "Who by searching can find out God." Job. xi. 7, 8, 9.

Q. What general knowledge have we of the character of God ?

A. That he conceived of all nature, material and immaterial, animate and inanimate, in heaven, earth, and worlds innumerable that fill the immensity of space, and by his almighty fiat spoke them into being.

Q. What particular knowledge have we of his character ?

A. That he regulates and controls all the events of the universe by his superintending

USE OF HISTORY.   7

Providence ; that the smallest, as well as the largest events are equally the objects of his care ; not a sparrow falls to the ground without his notice, and, even the hairs of our heads are all numbered.

Q. What evidence have we of this ?

A. The events predicted by the prophets, (through the inspiration of God,) and recorded in the sacred volume, hundreds and thousands of years before their accomplishment ; and the exact and particular accomplishment of those events, as recorded by historians, from the earliest ages of the world down to this day, all confirm this truth ; and further, that God regards all the particular parts of the universe as minutely as though there was but one ; and the whole with that general order and harmony, as if it had no parts.

Q. What is the use of history ?

A. To expand the mind of man, and lead it up to God ; as the great author, preserver, and governor of all things.

Q. What are we to understand by sacred history ?

A. That which relates to the church of God ; beginning with the call of Abraham, and continuing to the time of the Messiah, or CHRIST ; and from thence, to the end of the world.

Q. What are we to understand by profane history ?

A. A narrative of the transactions of men, generally, and individually ; comprising the rise and fall of nations, kingdoms, and empires.

Pages from Frederick Butler's *A General History of the World*. Like all early history texts, this work presents history from a providential perspective.

5. Take social action to preserve life, the family, liberty, and property; counsel government leaders about biblical positions on current issues — Perform Prophetic Function

We should speak out for biblical justice and take action to correct evil. This includes standing upon our legal rights and promoting and writing godly laws. The most significant civil documents bringing liberty to mankind were written by Christians or originated in Christian societies. Ministers in particular wrote many of these for they, being knowledgeable of the Bible—God's Law of Liberty—were best equipped to write civil laws of liberty. These included: Patrick's *Liber ex Lege Moise*, the Code of Justinian, King Alfred's Code of Laws, the Magna Carta by Rev. Stephen Langton, the Mayflower Compact by the Pilgrims, Fundamental Orders of Connecticut by Rev. Thomas Hooker, the Massachusetts Body of Liberties (the precursor to the U.S. Bill of Rights) by Rev. Nathaniel Ward, and the Frame of Government of Pennsylvania by William Penn.[130]

From the Old Testament prophets to the New Testament church leaders, God's people have taken action and counseled leaders: Nathan warned David, Elijah preached to Ahab, Daniel preached to Nebuchadnezzar, Moses warned Pharaoh, John the Baptist preached to Herod, and Jesus rebuked Herod. One way that church leaders performed a prophetic function in early America was via public sermons, through which they spoke to civil leaders as well as the nation at large.

Election Sermons

The Election Sermon was an annual event begun in 1633 in Massachusetts. Each year after elections were held, a minister was chosen to deliver an appropriate message to the newly elected officials and the gathered citizens. These discourses typically took place in the state house (which in Colonial America was usually the church meeting house; over time the states built their own government buildings). The Election Sermons were often printed and became their political textbooks. Historian John Wingate Thornton writes of the clergy's influence in early America:

> The clergy were generally consulted by the civil authorities; and not infrequently the suggestions from the pulpit, on election days and other

special occasions, were enacted into laws. The statute-book, the reflex of the age, shows this influence. The State was developed out of the Church.

The annual "Election Sermon" — a perpetual memorial, continued down through the generations from century to century — still bears witness that our fathers ever began their civil year and its responsibilities with an appeal to Heaven, and recognized Christian morality as the only basis of good laws....

The sermon is styled the *Election Sermon*, and is printed. Every representative has a copy for himself, and generally one or more for the minister or ministers of his town. As the patriots have prevailed, the preachers of each sermon have been the zealous friends of liberty; and the passages most adapted to promote the spread and love of it have been selected and circulated far and wide by means of newspapers, and read with avidity and a degree of veneration on account of the preacher and his election to the service of the day.[131]

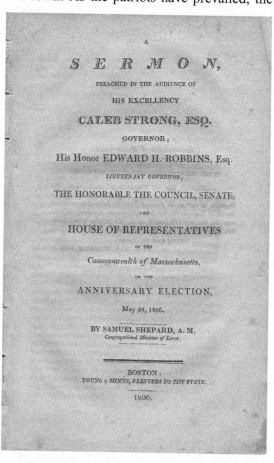

These election sermons were preached regularly in America for about 250 years (into the 1870's), and have been sporadically preached since then. Other public sermons also gave opportunity for ministers to perform their prophetic function in the nation.

Election Sermon preached before the government leaders in Massachusetts in 1806.

Fast and Thanksgiving Day Sermons

The first Americans were predominantly Christians who embraced the doctrine of Divine Providence, seeing God in history as "directly supervising the affairs of men, sending evil upon the city...for their sins...or blessing his people when they turn from their evil ways."[132] Looking to the Scriptures for the source of their law, both personal and civil, they firmly believed God's blessings would come upon those who obey His commands, and curses would come upon the disobedient (see Deuteronomy 28 and Leviticus 26). Consequently, during times of calamity or crisis both church and civil authorities would proclaim days of fasting and prayer; and when God responded with deliverance and blessing, they would proclaim days of thanksgiving and prayer. Such days of appeal to God were not rare, but a regular part of life in early America.

From 1620 to 1815 government (mostly colonial, and later state and national) proclaimed at least 1400 public days of fasting or thanksgiving. Such proclamations continued regularly throughout the nineteenth century, and in a

Possibly the first printed broadside for a Day of Prayer, September 8, 1670. Before this the numerous proclamations were written by hand.

smaller way up until today. During observances of fast and thanksgiving days, people would gather at their local meeting houses and churches to hear a sermon. State legislatures would also regularly invite ministers to preach on these days. Many of these sermons were printed and distributed for study.[133]

One example of a day of prayer occurred in October 1746 when France sent a fleet to attack Boston. Governor Shirley proclaimed a Fast Day and people everywhere thronged to the churches to pray for deliverance. God miraculously answered their prayers by sending a storm and pestilence to wipe out the French fleet. Everyone gave thanks to God.[134]

This not only occurred before independence, but also throughout the Revolution. During the Revolutionary War the Continental Congress issued at least seven different prayer and fast day proclamations and six different thanksgiving proclamations. These were issued after events such as the surrender of British General Burgoyne at Saratoga, the discovery of the treason of Benedict Arnold, and the surrender of Cornwallis at Yorktown. In response to the American victory at Saratoga in October 1777, the Continental Congress proclaimed a Day of Thanksgiving and Praise to God. They stated:

> Forasmuch as it is the indispensable duty of all men to adore the superintending providence of Almighty God,…and it having pleased Him in His abundant mercy…to crown our arms with most signal success…it is therefore recommended…to set apart Thursday, the 18th day of December, for solemn thanksgiving and praise.[135]

They recommended for everyone to confess their sins and humbly ask God, "through the merits of Jesus Christ, mercifully to forgive and blot them out of remembrance," and thus He then would be able to pour out His blessings upon every aspect of the nation.[136]

A Proclamation for a Day of Prayer issued by the Continental Congress in 1775.

The individual states proclaimed numerous such days as well. The Virginia House of Burgesses set apart June 1, 1774, as a day of fasting and prayer in response to England closing the port of Boston. On the day British troops fired upon the minutemen at Lexington (April 19, 1775) the colony of Connecticut was observing a "Day of publick Fasting and Prayer" as proclaimed a month before by Governor Trumbull. Massachusetts set aside August 1, 1776, as a "day of solemn humiliation, fasting, and prayer" where they called upon the people "to humble themselves under the righteous hand of God; penitently to acknowledge their many heinous and aggravated sins" and asking Him to "pour out of his Spirit upon this people…and that he would spread the peaceful Kingdom of the Divine Redeemer over the face of the whole habitable world."

TUESDAY, the 24th of MAY, 14 GEO. III. 1774.

THIS House being deeply impressed with Apprehension of the great Dangers to be derived to *British America*, from the hostile Invasion of the City of *Boston*, in our Sister Colony of *Massachusetts Bay*, whose Commerce and Harbour are on the 1st Day of *June* next to be stopped by an armed Force, deem it highly necessary that the said first Day of *June* be set apart by the Members of this House as a Day of Fasting, Humiliation and Prayer, devoutly to implore the divine Interposition for averting the heavy Calamity, which threatens Destruction to our civil Rights, and the Evils of civil War; to give us one Heart and one Mind firmly to oppose, by all just and proper Means, every Injury to *American* Rights, and that the Minds of his Majesty and his Parliament may be inspired from above with Wisdom, Moderation, and Justice, to remove from the loyal People of *America* all Cause of Danger from a continued Pursuit of Measures pregnant with their Ruin.

Ordered, therefore, that the Members of this House do attend in their Places at the Hour of ten in the Forenoon, on the said 1st Day of *June* next, in Order to proceed with the Speaker and the Mace to the Church in this City for the Purposes aforesaid ; and that the Reverend Mr. *Price* be appointed to read Prayers, and the Reverend Mr. *Gwatkin* to preach a Sermon suitable to the Occasion.

Ordered, that this Order be forthwith printed and published.

By the HOUSE of BURGESSES.

GEORGE WYTHE, C. H. B.

Thomas Jefferson, while a member of the Virginia legislature, penned this resolve for a day of fasting and prayer observed on June 1, 1774.

New York set aside August 27, 1776, "as a day of Fasting, Humiliation, and Prayer to Almighty God, for the imploring of His Divine assistance in the organization and establishment of a form of Government for the security and perpetuation of the Civil and Religious Rights and Liberties of Mankind."[137]

The modern separationists often look to Thomas Jefferson to justify their beliefs, saying he gave us separation of church and state. But Jefferson was no strict separationist, as shown by many of his public actions. He penned the resolve for Virginia's day of fasting and prayer on June 1, 1774. While Governor in 1779, he issued a proclamation "appointing Thursday the 9th day of December next, a day of publick and solemn thanksgiving and prayer to Almighty God, earnestly recommending to all the good people of this commonwealth, to set apart the said day for those purposes."[138]

If in session, Congress and the state assemblies would even go to church together as a body to observe these days. In 1787 a committee of representatives of all the states, gratefully looking back over all the preceding years, set apart October 19, 1787, "as a day of public prayer and thanksgiving" to their "all-bountiful Creator" who had conducted them "through the perils and dangers of the war" and established them as a free nation, and gave "them a name and a place among the princes and nations of the earth."[139]

The first President, George Washington, issued days of thanksgiving and days of prayer as recommended by Congress. Most Presidents up until today have followed this example, with about 200 such proclamations being issued by national government leaders.[140]

Also common in early America was the Artillery Sermon. These sermons were periodic addresses given to the military, especially during times of war, on such topics as "a defensive war in a just cause is sinless" and the sin of cowardice. Anniversary Sermons were preached in observance of victories, calamities, and special events. The church spoke God's truth to the nation through these public sermons.[141]

6. Endorse Godly civil leaders

The religious leaders in Israel often endorsed or confirmed the political leaders. As an example, Zadok the priest and Nathan the prophet anointed Solomon as king over Israel (1 Kings 1:34). The church should endorse godly leaders because, "When the righteous are in authority, the people rejoice, but when the wicked man rules, people groan" (Prov. 29:2).

In his *Lectures on Revival*, Charles Finney listed numerous things that were necessary for revival to continue in our nation. One of those items was:

> The Church must take right ground in regard to politics…. The time has come that Christians must vote for honest men, and take consistent ground in politics…or the country will be ruined. God cannot sustain this free and blessed country, which we love and pray for, unless the Church will take right ground. Politics are a part of a religion in such a country as this, and Christians must do their duty to the country as a part of their duty to God….He will bless or curse this nation, according to the course they [Christians] take [in politics].[142]

Charles Finney

7. Serve in positions of influence in the community and government as God directs — Perform Kingly Function

Many of God's people served in civil government in the Old Testament times, including Joseph, Moses, Joshua, the Judges, David, Solomon, Daniel, and many more. The New Testament also mentions Christians who served in government. Erastus was a part of Paul's missionary team until he sent him, along with Timothy, to Greece (Acts 19:22). Erastus remained at Corinth (2 Tim. 4:20) and while ministering to the churches there, he apparently felt called of God to serve in civil government, since Paul tells us in his letter to the Romans (written from Corinth) that Erastus had become the city treasurer (Rom. 16:23). Erastus had no problem moving from "pulpit" ministry to civil ministry. He was a minister, or servant, of God in both places (Rom. 13:4, 6).

Erastus exemplified Christian service well. A first-century tablet in Corinth contains the translated inscription: "Erastus, the Commissioner of Public Works, laid this pavement at his own expense." This is believed to be the Erastus of the Bible.[143]

Paul says that we will judge the world and angels, and if so, we must judge matters in this life (1 Cor. 6:1-6). Moreover, God has made us priests and kings (Rev. 1:6). We are called to rule and reign with him, not only in the future heaven and earth (ruling over cities is the reward of faithful stewards, Luke 19:17, 19), but in this present world as well. We have a kingly or governing function to perform. Of course, this is done in accordance with biblical standards as has been discussed in the previous chapters.

Many significant government leaders throughout history have been Christians. Some of those in America's history include George Washington, Samuel Adams, Patrick Henry, John Adams, George Mason, John Jay, James Madison, Noah Webster, John Quincy Adams, Daniel Webster, John Marshall, James Garfield, William McKinley, and myriads more.[144]

8. Be involved in selecting Godly officials

We have a duty to choose those who govern us because God holds us (and all men) responsible to establish and maintain righteous civil government, which is essential for His justice (Ex. 22:21-22; Isa. 1:16-17, 23; Jer. 5:28-29; 7:5-7; Mal. 3:5). When the righteous rule the people will rejoice, but when the wicked govern they will groan (Proverbs 29:2). Life is like a beautiful day when those who fear God rule (2 Samuel 23:3-4). Our nation's welfare and stability— our continuance as a nation of liberty, justice, and prosperity—will be greatly affected by those we choose to lead us in the legislative, judicial, and executive departments of state.

Practical ways to choose civil leaders

Four ways that you can participate in selecting those who govern are:
1) **Vote**
Voting is the minimal action we can take to fulfill our duty to establish and maintain righteous government. Sadly, today in America about one-half of those who claim to be Christians do not vote, thus giving over to secularists the exclusive role of choosing who rules them.

The Founders of America understood our duty to elect Christian men. John Jay, first Supreme Court Chief Justice, proclaimed: "Providence has given to our people the choice of their rulers, and it is the duty, as well as the privilege and interest, of our Christian nation, to select and prefer Christians for their rulers."[145]

If you live in a nation with no freedom to vote, then you can begin to pray, educate others, and act as prescribed in this book which, in conjunction with God's grace and plan, can bring the cultural change needed to implement this and others civil rights.

2) Support candidates

Identify people running for civil office that meet the biblical qualifications (see below) and support them in as many ways as possible, including financially, volunteering in their campaigns, educating the electorate on their qualities, etc.

3) Be involved in local party politics

The best way to know and choose candidates is consistent involvement in local party politics.

4) Run for office / start new political parties

If no godly candidates are running for office, consider running yourself. If no current political parties stand for righteousness, then consider starting a new political party. I have had the privilege of assisting in the establishment of a number of new political parties in other countries. Starting a party is difficult work requiring the cooperation of many people, but the benefits to society can be great. If there is no other recourse to have a voice in who governs you, then such a step may be essential.

Biblical Qualifications for Governing Officials

The qualifications of those who rule are of utmost importance. In choosing those who govern, we must compare their qualifications to those that the Bible says are of most importance.

If you could ask one question of a candidate for office to help you decide if you would vote for him, what would that question be? Many people would seek an answer to the question, "What are you going to do for me if you are elected?" The first time I voted in a presidential election was in 1972. This was before I became a Christian (in heart or head). I voted for the liberal losing candidate George McGovern because I thought his election would more enable me to live the immoral lifestyle that I pursued at that time. This is a typical motivation for many as they vote for those who govern.

Having put aside immorality, some Christians would ask candidates: Are you a Christian? Are you born again? Do you believe the Bible is the inspired word of God? Or any similar religious question. The answers to such questions are important; however, the answer can be positive but the person not be an effective ruler at all. By the 1976 election I had become a believer, though I lacked a biblical governmental worldview, and I considered this type of question to be most important. As I read about Jimmy Carter, the answer seemed "yes" for the questions above. He unashamedly spoke of being born again in *Time* magazine and I thought it would be great to have a Christian as President. While having some good qualities, Carter was not a good President. He did not govern in a biblical manner. He did not have the qualifications necessary to be a godly civil leader.

In the years following the 1976 election I began to grow in biblical knowledge and began to learn how to think governmentally. Now, in attempting to discern if a candidate is qualified to govern biblically, one question I would ask is: What is your philosophy of government? How a ruler governs is as important as the faith he proclaims. True biblical faith requires a biblical worldview.

Jimmy Carter may have been sincere in his claim as a born again Christian, but he was sincerely ignorant of biblical principles of government. His worldview, which affected his actions and policies, was more humanistic than biblical. That, coupled with a congress with the same worldview, produced the misery index, America held hostage (444 days), increased size and scope of civil government, and a movement of our nation toward more statism. His pagan philosophy of government did not help to bring liberty, justice and rejoicing by the people — the nation was not becoming more like "the light of the morning when the sun rises" (2 Sam. 23:3-4).

When Moses told the children of Israel to select from among them those who would govern them, he set forth a number of biblical qualifications. He said: "You shall select out of all the people, able men who fear God, men of truth, those who hate dishonest gain" (Ex. 18:21). "Choose wise and discerning and experienced men" (Deut. 1:13). He put forth three general qualifications for governing officials.[146]

1. Knowledge — "men of truth," "wise," "discerning"

As Matthias Burnet stated in an election sermon before the Connecticut Assembly in 1803, we should choose "men of good natural understanding and competent acquired knowledge."[147] Knowledge is more important than belief for daily living out your life. Many people say, "I believe in Christ," but this means different things for different people. Your knowledge determines your actions and belief, for as a man "thinks in his heart, so is he" (Prov. 23:7).

Some years ago I ruptured my Achilles tendon playing basketball. The first question I asked my family doctor about the various specialists who could perform surgery was, "who is best able to repair it?" not "which, if any, doctor is a Christian?" Now, if two were equally skilled, I would certainly choose the Christian.

The same concept applies to rulers. We want those who best know how to govern biblically — those who have a biblical philosophy of government. Some non-Christians' governmental philosophy is more biblical than some Christians'. Most rulers will not have all biblical qualifications, so we must weigh all factors. Mature Christians should have mature biblical knowledge. Unfortunately, many Christians never develop mature biblical knowledge. I would rather elect an unregenerate man with a biblical view of governance than a believer who thinks like a pagan, for your knowledge determines your actions.

Some people say that having a good heart and right intentions is of first importance. "If he means well, that is of most importance." Yet, if a man cannot discern the proper actions he is to take, he will always be in danger of being influenced by those who claim to be lovers of liberty and country, but are really more concerned with SELF and private interest; or he may be misguided in how to do good.

As an example, the Bible says we are to help the poor. To some Christians this means using the force of government to make everyone fulfill this duty. Those with this philosophy would tax all citizens and take this money to give to others. This is really socialism, justified under the guise of fulfilling our biblical duty. History has shown socialism does not work, and I believe that a study of the Scriptures reveals our duty to the poor must be fulfilled voluntarily by individual choice, and in a biblical manner.[148] Considering that one third of our tax dollars is spent on social programs, our rulers' governmental philosophy matters greatly.

The qualification of knowledge is not as the world sees knowledge. In a past presidential election one media leader argued that Al Gore was the better candidate because he had more knowledge — he went to Harvard, had a high IQ, and read a lot. Just being a knowledgeable person is not enough though. A ruler must have appropriate knowledge, related to fulfilling his duties. First, he must have a biblical philosophy of government, understanding the purpose of government, the premise of government, the power of government, jurisdictional authority, and the other ideas we covered in the previous chapters.

Other aspects of a biblical philosophy of government that godly leaders should embrace include being pro-life, pro-liberty, and pro-property rights; having knowledge of inalienable rights, the laws of nature, and the laws of nature's God; and knowing the U.S. and their state Constitutions. Today, most of our rulers have a limited knowledge of the Constitution, especially the original intent. Leaders should understand the power and form of free nations[149] and that self-government under God is the foundation of all earthly government. Having an understanding of principles is more important than holding certain views on issues because a man trained in fundamental biblical governmental principles and a biblical philosophy of government will know how to reason to specific issues.

It is also important for godly leaders to have knowledge of specific application of civil law. They should understand God's civil laws and how they apply. For example, understanding and applying the appropriate penalties God sets forth in the Bible for violating criminal law would alleviate many of our criminal problems today.

The governmental philosophy of officials is important. This determines their position on specific issues and on what laws they will enact, or not enact, how they will spend tax dollars, how they will protect the law-abiding citizens, et cetera. But knowledge in itself is not enough. They also need wisdom to apply the spirit of the law.

Wisdom to Apply Knowledge and Skill in Governing

Solomon received from God a wise and an understanding heart, which was necessary for him to be able to govern well. In general he brought much good to the nation, but he also displayed wisdom in specific judgments. Solomon's judgment in the situation of the women arguing over the baby is an excellent example of godly wisdom. Godly rulers need such wisdom.

Godly officials will be "able and experienced men" — they will be skillful. Effective rulers will have the specific knowledge, talents, and skills necessary to fulfill their specific governing roles. For example, a president needs executive skills, which may differ from skills needed to be a congressman or a judge.

Good leaders will also educate their constituents. King Josiah read the Scriptures (the law, the covenant, the constitution) to all the people to inform them of how to live. As a result "all the people took a stand for the covenant" (2 Kings 23:2-3). Rulers can and should do this today; that is, educate folks in biblical truth as it applies to their function in civil society, and also educate folks in the Constitution and laws of the nation.

Officials may have correct knowledge, but they need something much more to assure they will act upon what they know to be right, and that they will resist the temptations that come with power and influence. They need godly character to assure they will govern rightly and with humility.

2. Morality or Christian Character — "men of truth," "hate dishonest gain"

A second qualification for godly officials is morality. They should be "men truly honest and upright in their principles and views, not actuated and governed by the sordid motives of self interest and aggrandizement in their desire and execution of office, but by a sincere regard to the public good."[150]

There are many examples in history where corrupt and unprincipled rulers (such as Hitler, Stalin, Idi Amin) have brought on all kinds of miseries to mankind—including loss of liberty and the downfall of nations. Chandler Robbins, in an election sermon in 1791, said, "Nothing will so surely, so rapidly bring on the dissolution of society, and the loss of the liberties of a people, as a want of virtue and integrity in their rulers."[151]

Like all men, civil leaders will be exposed to temptations, but perhaps to greater temptations than most since they are in a position to wield great power. They contend with flattery to divert them from the right course. They must practice self-denial and lay aside their self-interest and private concerns for the betterment of society at large. They must deal with the fear of man and the pressure that comes when many people and groups are pushing them in a certain way. "Firmness of mind is therefore necessary to repel these and a thousand other temptations."[152] Good leaders must have "firmness and fortitude of soul arising from principle, and cultivated with care."[153] Other character qualities needed by rulers include:

Honesty / Integrity

Honesty is obviously important in a ruler. Proverbs 29:12 says "if a ruler pays attention to falsehood [hearkens to lies], all his ministers become wicked." If a man cannot keep personal vows or oaths, we cannot expect him to keep national vows. We have witnessed this in recent years.

Knowledge or intelligence (as man sees it) without honesty — a good genius with a bad heart — is worse than an ignorant honest man because the evil genius could find more subtle ways to rob the people of their rights. Some have argued support for certain candidates based upon their intelligence, saying: "He's so smart. We ought to elect him." Yet, if a man, no matter how smart, is reasoning from wrong presuppositions, or has bad character, he will not be a good leader.

Just and Compassionate

We need rulers with firmness and resolution, yet also with compassion, tenderness, and kindness. As a "minister of God" he should imitate the "Father of mercies." God is merciful, but He is also just and righteous. When such a ruler inflicts punishment on offenders, he "does it, not because he takes pleasure in the misery of his subjects, but to vindicate his authority and government — to preserve order in the system, and, in the end, to promote the public good."[154] This is the emphasis of biblical law — restitution to the wronged and restoration of godly order — and is in contrast to the Roman idea of law which seeks firstly the punishment of the criminal. The Roman idea is much more pronounced in our penal system today.

Humility

Jesus taught that leaders are to be servants (Matt. 20:25-28). George Washington understood this as evidenced by a letter he sent to all the Governors, on June 8, 1783, where he gave the following advice:

> I now make it my earnest prayer, that God would have you, and the State over which you preside, in his holy protection....that he would most graciously be pleased to dispose us all to do justice, to love mercy, and to demean ourselves with that charity, humility, and pacific temper of mind, which were the characteristics of the Divine Author of our blessed religion, and without an humble imitation of whose example in these things, we can never hope to be a happy nation.[155]

George Washington

Washington was a great example of a humble leader. His response to and rejection of the proposition by some officers in the army to make him king is one incident showing this.[156]

3. Faith or True Religion — "men who fear God"

The fear of God is an essential qualification for a godly official. What are men like who fear God? "Men acting under the belief and awe of God as their inspector and judge, to whom they consider themselves accountable for their conduct and whom they fear to offend."[157]

This is not just saying "I am a Christian," simply going to church, or culturally embracing Christianity, but having a reverential fear of the Almighty. Many today think that the fear of God is of no matter for our rulers, and even see it as a negative factor. Rev. Matthias Burnet expressed well why a fear of God is important:

> If God be such a being, as both reason and revelation declare him to be, an omniscient, holy, just and all-powerful being, whose eyes are in every place, beholding the evil and the good, to punish the one and reward the other according to their character and deeds, then certainly, the fear and awe of him must operate as the greatest restraint from that which is evil, and the most powerful incentive to that which is good, and he who is truly actuated by this principle, will never give his voice or influence to pervert justice or support iniquity. But the man who does not believe in the being and providence of God, or is not actuated by the fear and awe of him, has in many cases no bond or restraint upon his conduct, and therefore is not fit to be trusted with a nation's weal, which he will not scruple, whenever he can with impunity, to sacrifice to his lust or ambition.[158]

When the righteous rule the people rejoice (Prov. 29:2). The righteous are those in right standing with God — they fear God. Rev. Robbins preached to the Massachusetts officials in 1791:

> By a man of Religion, I mean one who fears God from the heart, with a fear founded in esteem — in a supreme love implanted in the soul, by the renovating influence of the Spirit of God — one who believes in, and honors his Son Jesus Christ, as the only mediator and Saviour; and who makes conscience of conforming his temper and life to the sacred rules of the Gospel.[159]

Early Americans looked for this quality in their rulers, and most rulers were men who feared God. Men who lacked, or were hostile to, true religion would not be tolerated. Irreligion in a ruler counteracts the design of the office to execute justice. A leader who does not fear God will not make an effective governor, for if he himself disregards the laws of God, how can he effectively condemn the vice and immorality of others? If he is a slave to his lusts, how can he attempt to regulate the passions of others. In so doing, people will cry out, "Physician heal thyself." All authority will be brought into contempt. We have seen this negative effect today, with some citizens justifying lying, and many other things, in personal actions because some officials did the same thing.

Righteous rulers are called of God and have vision.

The book of Romans, Chapter 13, tells us that civil rulers are ministers of God who hold their position by His providence. It is a ministry that God will call some people to fill. We should discern if those we seek to place in power are those that God has called and "anointed" to rule. God prepares different people to perform different things. Recognizing the call of God on a person for a specific office is important. There are many examples in history of God's call on rulers, including David, Moses, Daniel, William Penn, and George Washington.

Having a godly vision for administering God's justice in the civil realm is important for effective leadership. A godly leader will have knowledge, Christian character, and a fear of God and will be able to impart vision, hope, purpose, and direction to a nation. This is especially true for those in executive positions like presidents, governors, and mayors. Godly rulers will use the office as a "pulpit" to raise the vision of the American people and implant noble desires and hope for the future.

Noah Webster clearly explained the effect of unprincipled men in office:

> Let it be impressed on your mind that God commands you to choose for yourselves rulers, "just men who rule in the fear of God." The preservation of a republican government depends on the faithful discharge of this duty; if the citizens neglect their duty and place unprincipled men in office, the government will soon be corrupted; laws will be made, not for the public good, so much as for selfish or local purposes; corrupt or incompetent men will be appointed to execute the laws; the public revenues will be squandered on unworthy men; and the rights of the citizens will be violated or disregarded. If a republican government fails to secure public prosperity and happiness, it must be because the citizens neglect the divine commands, and elect bad men to make and administer the laws.[160]

Noah Webster

The election of unprincipled men produces misery and tyranny, but godly rulers bring peace, prosperity, justice, and rejoicing. If we fulfill our duty and place godly men in office (who have knowledge, character, and faith) our future will be bright. According to 2 Samuel 23:3-4, "The God of Israel said…He who rules…in the fear of God, is as the light of the morning when the sun rises, a morning without clouds, when the tender grass springs out of the earth, through sunshine after rain."

Chapter 11

Conclusion

Involvement in Government and Politics

Should Christians be involved in politics, government, and the public affairs of our nation? Some pastors say that it is okay for you to be involved if you feel called of God to do so, but not everyone is. Being involved is a matter of Christian liberty, they say, where some may take action and others not, depending upon your conscience and calling. However, I would argue (along with many Christian leaders throughout history) that it is not just biblically permissible for us to be involved in government as Christians, but is it our duty. And as we have seen, our biblical civil duties are quite extensive.

In truth, anyone who is committed to obeying the Bible will be involved in politics—politics meaning, "that which deals with the regulation and government of a nation or state, for the preservation of its safety, peace, and prosperity"—because about 70% of the Bible deals with social, political, and national issues, while only 30% deals with personal affairs. We cannot be involved with advancing the Kingdom of God in history without being involved in politics. God gave mankind a big mission, and He gave us all we need to accomplish that mission. We are not left to follow secular political scientists regarding how to govern. God has "granted to us everything pertaining to life and godliness" (2 Pet. 1:3).

In general, we have a duty to learn what the Bible says about government and then to act upon what it says. Families, churches, and Christian schools have a duty to teach a biblical view of politics. Pastors must not only instruct their churches regarding their biblical civil duties, but they must once again become watchmen on the walls and warn the church and the nation of the action of the enemies of God to usurp Christ's kingship over His earth and our role as vice-regents, ruling in His place.

Some people will be called to be political philosophers instructing the rulers of the earth how to govern in a biblical way, and thus laying the foundation for free, just, virtuous, and prosperous nations. Others will be called to serve in government, ruling in the fear of God and with godly wisdom. In short, God's people must perform their Levitical, prophetic, and kingly functions.

Liberty: the Fruit of Biblical Government

God's intent for giving us principles of government is to help us live in liberty. Christ came to liberate man (Gal. 5:1). He came to proclaim liberty to the oppressed (Luke 4:18). One purpose of civil government is to protect that great liberty that comes to mankind via the Gospel. All men have liberty before the law of God — religious, civil, and economic liberty. Liberty is having freedom to do God's will, rather than having freedom to do my will (whatever I want to do). Montesquieu says liberty "consists in the power of doing what we ought to will, and in not being constrained to do what we ought not to will."[161]

God delivered Israel from slavery to freedom, while Christ delivers His covenant people all over the world. Montesquieu said that countries are not cultivated in proportion to their fertility, but to their liberty. They do not prosper according to their natural resources, but their degree of liberty. God's Law and system of government gave great liberty to Israel, which in turn produced great prosperity. God's Law and polity will bring liberty to any nation embracing them. As Signer of the U.S. Declaration Benjamin Rush wrote, "Christianity is the only true and perfect religion, and that in proportion as mankind adopt its principles and obeys its precepts, they will be wise and happy."[162]

As mankind adopts His principles and obeys His precepts they will have liberty, happiness, justice, and great blessings. His principles are for all of life, including public affairs. Since God is king of all creation and ruler of all the earth we should obey Him. But God also wants us to obey Him for our well-being. His principles of government are a matrix of liberty that we must apply in the earth to help bring forth His kingdom here as it is in heaven.

PP

About the Author

 Stephen McDowell is co-founder and President of the Providence Foundation, a nonprofit Christian educational organization whose mission is to train leaders of education, business, and politics to transform their culture for Christ. After obtaining a B.S. Degree in physics at the University of North Carolina at Chapel Hill and a M.S. Degree in geology at the University of Memphis, he was ordained for the ministry in 1978, working in the pastorate until 1984 when he assisted in establishing the Providence Foundation.

McDowell is the editor of the *Providential Perspective* and has authored or co-authored over 40 books, videos, and training courses, including *America's Providential History, Liberating the Nations, Building Godly Nations, In God We Trust Tour Guide, Transforming Nations through Biblical Work*, and *Apostle of Liberty: The World-Changing Leadership of George Washington.* His study, *Monumental: Restoring America as the Land of Liberty*, was done in conjunction with Kirk Cameron as a follow-up course to Cameron's *Monumental* film. *The Bible: America's Source of Law and Liberty* has been distributed to members of state legislators in 20 states with the goal of reaching all 50. Stephen's books and writings have been translated into 18 languages and distributed to over one million people.

He has traveled throughout the United States and to 40 nations in six continents, teaching tens of thousands of people from more than 100 different countries. He has consulted with numerous government officials, assisted in writing political documents and starting political parties, established classes on godly reformation in numerous churches, and helped start a number of Christian schools.

McDowell has been an Adjunct Professor at Regent University, has written scores of articles for various publications, appeared on numerous TV and radio programs (including the Glenn Beck show and Fox & Friends), contributed articles to *The Founders' Bible*, appeared in the *Monumental* film, and spoken to many different religious, educational, civic, and political organizations. He also periodically does historic portrayals of Thomas Jefferson. He and his wife Beth live in Charlottesville, Virginia, and have four children and six grandchildren.

About the Providence Foundation

Discipling the Nations ♦ Restoring America as the Land of Liberty

The Providence Foundation is a Christian educational organization whose mission is to train leaders to transform their culture for Christ, and to teach all citizens how to disciple nations. We have been working since our founding in 1984 to fulfill Christ's commission to "make disciples of all nations." Such nations will have transformed people, but also transformed institutions – family, church, and state.

We have focused on training in a principled, biblical education that has historically produced liberty, justice, prosperity, virtue, and knowledge in people and nations.

The Providence Foundation provides training and produces resources necessary for pastors, teachers, government leaders, businessmen, parents, and students to live and think Biblically, and to equip others to disciple the nations.

- We have produced scores of different books, audios, videos, and courses in 18 different languages with over 2 million being distributed around the world.
- We have trained tens of thousands of people from over 100 countries.
- We have consulted with leaders who have started political parties, Christian schools, organizations, and reformational groups.
- We have representatives throughout the USA and around the world who are educating others and working to bring godly reform.
- We offer over 50 different seminars, presentations, and talks, with staff and representatives speaking to thousands of churches, schools, home-school groups, social and political organizations, radio and TV outlets.

To arrange a speaker or for more information contact:

Providence Foundation, PO Box 6759, Charlottesville, VA 22906
Website: providencefoundation.com   Phone: 434-978-4535
Email: info@providencefoundation.com

What Others Have Said

"America as well as nations across the world have benefited from the principles of Godly government that the Providence Foundation teaches both to citizens and government officials. I highly commend their important work."
David Barton, President, WallBuilders

"I am SOOO thankful for you and the Providence Foundation's ministry. Your booklets are tremendous and my favorite educational tools. I feel desperate to get their principles into the hands of the nation. Keep up the great work!" – **Kirk Cameron**, Actor

"*America's Providential History* had a life changing effect on me. God has spoken to my heart to share this book at our conferences and make it available to other Christians so that they may obtain knowledge and become aware of their Christian heritage and experience the effect of it in their lives."
Dave Meyer, Life in the Word / Joyce Meyer Ministries

"I just finished studying your booklet, *The Threat of Islam to liberty and Christianity*. It is a fine piece of scholarship that merits the widest distribution possible. It is a first rate summary of the history and interaction of Christianity and Islam. Your handling of the Crusades is the most succinct I have read anywhere. Congratulations, very well done." – **General Jerry Curry** (Ret.)

"This latest book by Stephen McDowell is a great resource for anyone who desires to know the true source of law and liberty in America. For decades, American Family Association has worked to restore biblical values in our culture and this book by Stephen is a great tool to do just that."
Tim Wildmon, President, American Family Association

"If you are a leader, Stephen McDowell's book, *The Bible: America's Source of Law and Liberty*, is absolutely essential knowledge. On our shoulders rests the future of the greatness of our nation. Read this! Finish it. Read it again. Retain it. Teach it until it is retained!"
Kevin Jones, Kansas State Representative, 5th District, Former US Army Green Beret

Providence Foundation Resources

Biblical Worldview University
Training Leaders to Transform Their Culture for Christ

Order these books, courses, and other resources today:

providencefoundation.com
434-978-4535
info@providencefoundation.com

End Notes

[1] James L. Garlow and David Barton, *This Precarious Moment, Six Urgent Steps that Will Save You, Your Family, and Our Country*, Salem Books, 2018, pp. 218-219.

[2] Developing a biblical worldview is important for every area of life. For example, as we approach child training and discipline we need to know about having biblical attitudes toward our children, but parents also need guidance on how to provide biblical discipline. Christians have different views on how to train and discipline children, just as they have different views on government. That being so does not mean the church should avoid the subject and let everyone decide on their own how to act. If the church does not have a clear biblical position on certain topics or recognizes God allows for liberty on certain issues, the church should at least teach a variety of views in order to give believers a framework to evaluate and choose. The problem of some churches is they will not teach on the subject at all and, hence, many folks have no access to ideas to form a conviction.

[3] Jonathan Mayhew "A Discourse Concerning Unlimited Submission and Non-Resistance to the Higher Powers," Boston: Printed by D. Fowle and D. Gookin, 1750, John Wingate Thornton, *The Pulpit of the American Revolution*, Boston: Gould and Lincoln, 1860, pp. 47, 53-54.

[4] The author presupposes that the Bible is the divine, inspired, inerrant Word of the living God. For proof of this foundational Christian belief see Stephen McDowell, *The Bible, Divine or Human? Evidence of Biblical Infallibility and Support for Building Your Life and Nation on Biblical Truth,* Charlottesville: Providence Foundation, 2016. In addition, the author believes the Bible gives guidance for all areas of life, including civil government, and that we have a duty to find out what God says about government and then seek to act upon His Word.

[5] See books by Stephen McDowell: *God's Blueprint for Life, Liberty, and Property*; *The Ten Commandments and Modern Society*; *Equal Justice Under God's Law, Building Nations with the Blueprint of God's Word*; *Crime and Punishment: A Biblical Perspective*, all published by Providence Foundation, Charlottesville, Virginia.

[6] See for example: E.C. Wines, *The Hebrew Republic*, Uxbridge, Mass.: American Presbyterian Press, 1980; Rousas John Rushdoony, *The Institutes of Biblical Law*, The Presbyterian and Reformed Publishing Co., 1973; Robert Fugate, *Key Biblical Principles for Civil Government*, Omaha: The Word of Truth Publishers, 2007; John Eidsmoe, *Historical and Theological Foundations of Law, 3 Vols.*, Powder Springs, Ga: American Vision Press, 2011; Greg L. Bahnsen, *By This Standard, The Authority of God's Law Today*, Tyler, Tex.: Institute for Christian Economics, 1985; Rus Walton, *Biblical Solutions to Contemporary Problems: A Handbook*, Brentwood, Tenn.: Wolgemuth & Hyatt, 1988; *Biblical Blueprint Series*, Gary North, editor, Ft. Worth: Dominion Press, 1987; *Rebuilding Civilization on the Bible*, Jay Grimstead and Coalition on Revival, Ventura, Cal.: Nordskog Publishing, 2014.

[7] For more on capital punishment see Stephen McDowell, *Crime and Punishment, A Biblical Perspective*, Charlottesville: Providence Foundation, 2011.

[8] Noah Webster, *An American Dictionary of the English Language*, republished in facsimile edition by Foundation for American Christian Education, San Francisco, 1980. Definition of *government*.

[9] Quoted in Rosalie J. Slater, *Teaching and Learning America's Christian History*, San Francisco: Foundation for American Christian Education, 1980, p. 119.

[10] The complete civil code and set of laws affecting Americans today are so vast it would take about 25,000 years for one person to read them all (and who knows how many of those laws and policies each of us is violating). Secular man governs via an ever-increasing number of external laws, and he calls it liberty. God gives man ten general principles by which to live, writes His

laws on man's heart, and empowers him with the Holy Spirit to desire and be able to live by those principles. God's way is true liberty.

[11] Robert C. Winthrop, "Address to Massachusetts Bible Society Meeting, May 28, 1849," *Addresses and Speeches on Various Occasions*, Boston: Little, Brown & Co., 1852, p. 172.

[12] *Maxims of Washington*, compiled by John Frederick Schroeder, New York: D. Appleton & Co., 1854, p. 341.

[13] Noah Webster, *A Manual of Useful Studies*, New Haven: S. Babcock, 1839, pp. 77-78.

[14] For more on the family see Stephen McDowell, *The Biblical Family: Instrument of Godly Transformation*, Charlottesville: Providence Foundation, 2015.

[15] It is beyond the scope of this book to deal with forms of church government. Some general thoughts can be found in Mark Beliles and Stephen McDowell, *America's Providential History*, Charlottesville: Providence Foundation, 2010, pp. 78-79.

[16] Rosalie J. Slater, *Teaching and Learning America's Christian History*, San Francisco: Foundation for American Christian Education, 1980, p. 40.

[17] For more see Stephen McDowell, *Transforming Nations through Biblical Work*, Charlottesville: Providence Foundation, 2018.

[18] While man's sinful heart is the primary motive for evil action, there are numerous secondary reasons that may provoke some men to commit crimes and atrocities, including bad company, evil environment, and corruption. However, one's external circumstances are never justification for sinful and criminal behavior (as God defines criminal). Changing the external circumstances, no matter how bad, are not sufficient to deal with the source of evil behavior.

[19] John Adams, *The Works of John Adams*, Charles Francis Adams, editor (Boston: Little, Brown & Co., 1856), Vol. 6, A Defense of the Constitutions of Government of the United States of America, "Chapter First. Marchamont Nedham. The Right Constitution of a Commonwealth Examined."

[20] Alexander Hamilton, James Madison, and John Jay, *The Federalist, A Commentary on the Constitution of the United States*, edited by Paul Leicester Ford, New York: Henry Holt and Company, 1898, p. 344.

[21] Charles Clay, *An Artillery Sermon on The Governor Among the Nations*, c. 1777, contained in the Clay Family Papers (Mss 1c5795a), Virginia Historical Society, Richmond, Virginia.

[22] Milton E. Flower, *John Dickinson Conservative Revolutionary*, Charlottesville: The University Press of Virginia, 1983, p. 67.

[23] *Maxims of Washington*, compiled by John Frederick Schroeder, New York: D. Appleton & Co., 1854, p. 352.

[24] Noah Webster, *History of the United States*, New Haven: Durrie & Peck, 1833, pp. 273-274.

[25] This cry for freedom arises primarily in a Christian people or where Christian ideas affect society. Sin deadens the conscience of man and diminishes his quest for true freedom.

[26] Charles Hodge, *Commentary on the Epistle to the Romans*, Revised edition. New York: Armstrong, 1893, p. 639. In Rousas John Rushdoony, *Politics of Guilt and Pity*, Vallecito, Cal.: Ross House Books, 1995, p. 336.]

[27] Samuel West, *A Sermon Preached before the Honorable Council, and the Honorable House of Representatives of the Colony of Massachusetts-Bay in New-England, May 29th, 1776*, Boston: Printed by John Gill, 1776, in John Wingate Thornton, *The Pulpit of the American Revolution*, Boston: Gould and Lincoln, 1860, pp. 283-284.

[28] Jonathan Mayhew "A Discourse Concerning Unlimited Submission and Non-Resistance to the Higher Powers," Boston: Printed by D. Fowle and D. Gookin, 1750, In Thornton, pp. 39-104.

[29] Hodge, p. 641, in Rushdoony, p. 337.

[30] For more on this see Stephen McDowell, *Crime and Punishment: A Biblical Perspective*, Charlottesville: Providence Foundation, 2011.

[31] See McDowell, *Crime and Punishment*.

[32] Matthew Henry's *Commentary on the Whole Bible*, Hendrickson Publishers, 2002, Rom.13:1-7, pp. 2229-2231.

[33] Thomas Jefferson, *Notes on the State of Virginia*, Trenton: Printed by Wilson & Blackwell, 1803, p. 222.

[34] See Stephen McDowell, *The Economy from a Biblical Perspective*, Charlottesville: Providence Foundation, 2009, pp. 9-13.

[35] Prohibition was passed with the laudable goal of reducing drunkenness and its bad effects. Consuming alcohol is not sinful in itself, though excess consumption is a sin, as the Bible repeatedly warns against this. Drunkenness can lead to criminal behavior and it would be legitimate for governments to declare some related behavior as criminal, such as drunk driving. The ultimate solution to drunkenness is transformation of the heart and mind of men by the power and truth of God.

[36] See McDowell, *Crime and Punishment*.

[37] For an expansion on these duties, see McDowell, *Crime and Punishment* and Robert Fugate, *Key Principles for Civil Government*, Omaha: Thy Word Is Truth Publishers, p. 29 ff.

[38] For an overview of biblical precepts for 21 areas of life see Stephen McDowell, *Equal Justice Under God's Law, Building Nations with the Blueprint of God's Word*, Charlottesville: Providence Foundation, 2010.

[39] The code of Hammurabi was harsh; for example, it required death for stealing in some cases: "If any one steal cattle or sheep, or an ass, or a pig or a goat, if it belong to a god or to the court, the thief shall pay thirtyfold; if they belonged to a freed man of the king he shall pay tenfold; if the thief has nothing with which to pay he shall be put to death." "If anyone commits a robbery and is caught, he shall be put to death." There are many other penalties like these that are not commensurate with the crime. Also, it did not provide liberty or justice for all. The code emanated from the king, who was the highest authority. The flow of power in this society was from the top down.

[40] For more on the kingdom, see Stephen McDowell, *The Kingdom of God*, Charlottesville: Providence Foundation, 2012.

[41] See McDowell, *Crime and Punishment*.

[42] *Sources of Our Liberty, Documentary Origins of Individual Liberties in the United States Constitution and Bill of Rights*, edited by Richard L. Perry, American Bar Foundation, 1952, p. 60.

[43] Lord Acton, quoted in John Eidsmoe, *Historical and Theological Foundations of Law, Vol. 1, Ancient Wisdom*, Powder Springs, Ga.: American Vision Press, 2012, p. 474.

[44] Augustus Neander, *General History of the Christian Religion and Church*, quoted in Rosalie Slater, *Teaching and Learning America's Christian History*, San Francisco: Foundation for American Christian Education, 1980, p. 213.

[45] Ibid., p. 214.

[46] God's Law is not abrogated by the New Covenant. The New Testament contains over 1600 citations of the Old Testament, including about 300 direct quotes. It reaffirms the moral law of God, and even many case laws, citing over 20. Under the New Covenant the laws of God are maintained unless modified. Some modifications include: Christ's fulfillment of the ceremonial laws, the Christian Sabbath superseding the Hebrew Sabbath, and holiness code laws modified by the spiritual nature of God's new covenant nation.

[47] To understand more fully Christ and the law of God, see Stephen McDowell, *God's Blueprint for Life, Liberty, and Property*, Charlottesville: Providence Foundation, 2014, pp. 16-17.

[48] The Christian Sabbath would modify the Hebrew Sabbath, and so Jesus did not directly teach upholding all the Hebrew Sabbath with its penalties. He did point out how the Pharisees had perverted the law regarding the Hebrew Sabbath.

[49] See McDowell, *Crime and Punishment*.

[50] To help in understanding this incident consider: Jesus was not a civil authority and would not make himself a judge in legal affairs. Any judge had to have clean hands regarding the crime

over which they sat in judgment, and those scribes and Pharisees apparently did not. Jesus upheld the biblical requirement of having 2 or 3 witnesses. He could not pronounce guilt without this. Jesus pronounced religious forgiveness, not civil forgiveness. Additionally, Israel did not enforce the death penalty for adultery at this time because the Roman authorities prohibited them to do so. Thus, the Pharisees were obviously trying to embarrass Him. Finally, if she was caught in the act, where was the man? Why was he not being charged along with the woman?

[51] Samuel West in Thornton, p. 284.

[52] Emigration is leaving a country, which all men should have the freedom to do. Immigration is coming to a country of which one is not a resident. Who can immigrate into a nation is not to be decided by the immigrant, but by the government of that country.

[53] See Stephen McDowell and Mark Beliles, *Liberating the Nations*, Chapter 13.

[54] John Jay, Letter to John Murray, April 15, 1818, in *In God We Trust, The Religious Beliefs and Ideas of the American Founding Fathers*, edited by Norman Cousins, New York: Harper & Brothers, 1958, p. 369.

[55] The purpose of civil government was covered in more detail in Chapter 4.

[56] The Bible teaches that all capital crimes, except willful murder, could have lesser penalties. Death was a maximum penalty. For example: Non-premeditated manslaughter (Ex. 21:28-32; ransom paid); false witness in capital crime (Deut. 22:18-19; 19:16-20; Lev. 20:10); treason (1 Kings 1:52-53). God built flexibility into His law to make it restorative (Ezek. 18). Governing authorities and victims of the crime had the ability to consider any extenuating circumstances.

[57] See McDowell, *Crime and Punishment*, for an explanation of these penalties.

[58] For more biblical arguments for limited government see Elisha Williams' "Essential Rights and Liberties of Protestants." Portions of this 1744 pamphlet are published in *America's Providential History, A Documentary Sourcebook*, Stephen McDowell, editor, Charlottesville: Providence Foundation, 2004, pp. 32-38.

[59] See Stephen McDowell, *The Ten Commandments and Modern Society*, Charlottesville: Providence Foundation, 1999.

[60] John Cotton, *An Exposition upon the Thirteenth Chapter of the Revelation*, p. 72; quoted in Rousas John Rushdoony, *Politics of Guilt and Pity*, Vallecito, Cal.: Ross House Books, 1995, p. 162.

[61] John Adams, *The Works of John Adams*, Charles Francis Adams, editor (Boston: Little, Brown & Co., 1856), Vol. 6, *A Defense of the Constitutions of Government of the United States of America*, "Chapter First. Marchamont Nedham. The Right Constitution of a Commonwealth Examined."

[62] Rousas John Rushdoony, *The Institutes of Biblical Law*, The Presbyterian and Reformed Publishing Co., 1973, p.612.

[63] Massachusetts Body of Liberties, *Sources of Our Liberties*, Richard L. Perry, editor, New York: American Bar Foundation, 1952, p. 148.

[64] Rushdoony, p. 612.

[65] James Madison, No. 39, *The Federalist, A Commentary on the Constitution of the United States*, New York: Henry Holt and Company, 1898, p. 245.

[66] Stephen McDowell, *No Cross, No Crown, The Life Message of William Penn*, Charlottesville: Providence Foundation, 2017, p. 16.

[67] Elias Boudinot, "Oration at Elizabethtown, New Jersey, on the Fourth of July, 1793." *American Eloquence: A Collection of Speeches and Addresses, by the Most Eminent Orators of America*, 1:265.

[68] *Christian History of the Constitution of the United States*, compiled by Verna M. Hall, San Francisco: Foundation for American Christian Education, 1908, pp. 16-17.

[69] E.C. Wines, *The Hebrew Republic*, Uxbridge, Mass.: American Presbyterian Press, 1980, p. 53.

[70] The three annual festivals in Israel contributed to the union as well, since all the men and many women from all 12 tribes would unite around a common time of worship and learning.

[71] For more on this see, McDowell, *Crime and Punishment*.

[72] Wines, *The Hebrew Republic*, p. 8.

[73] Rosalie J. Slater, "Noah Webster, Founding Father of American Scholarship and Education," article in Preface of the facsimile reprint of Noah Webster, *An American Dictionary of the English Language*, p. 14.

[74] Wines, *The Hebrew Republic*, p. 9.

[75] John Locke, *Of Civil Government*, quoted in *Christian History of the Constitution*, p. 58.

[76] Wines, p. 29.

[77] Wines, p. 40.

[78] Wines, pp. 33-34.

[79] Similarly, America's holidays (which were holy days originally) are a potential means of learning about God's history and truth (see https://providencefoundation.com/category/americas-holidays/).

[80] Wines, p. 46.

[81] Slater, *Teaching and Learning*, p. 251.

[82] *Frame of Government of Pennsylvania*, April 25, 1682, "The Preface," in *Sources of Our Liberties*, Richard L. Perry, editor, New York: American Bar Foundation, 1952, pp. 210-211.

[83] See Stephen McDowell, *The Bible: America's Source of Law and Liberty*, Charlottesville: Providence Foundation, 2015.

[84] B.F. Morris, *Christian Life and Character of the Civil Institutions of the United States*, Philadelphia: George W. Childs, 1864, p. 270.

[85] For an examination of God's laws of liberty see Stephen McDowell, *The Ten Commandments and Modern Society* and *God's Blueprint for Life, Liberty, and Property*.)

[86] Wines' Book II has been reprinted as: E.C. Wines, *The Hebrew Republic*, Uxbridge, Mass.: American Presbyterian Press, 1980.

[87] Wines, p. 101.

[88] See Wines, pp. 101-102, 105-107.

[89] See Wines, pp. 148 ff.

[90] See Wines, pp. 196-197.

[91] For more, see Chapter 10 and Stephen McDowell, "Qualifications for Godly Officials," *Building Godly Nations*, Charlottesville: Providence Foundation, 2003, pp. 231-247.

[92] For more on the Ten Commandments and God's law see Stephen McDowell, *The Ten Commandments and Modern Society*, and *God's Blueprint for Life, Liberty, and Property*.

[93] For four opinions of what they were, see Wines, pp. 210-211.

[94] Wines, p. 221.

[95] See Stephen McDowell, *The Bible: America's Source of Law and Liberty*, Charlottesville: Providence Foundation, 2015.

[96] See Chapter 10 as well as Beliles and McDowell, *America's Providential History*, Chapters 8 and 9.

[97] See McDowell, *The Kingdom of God*. Wines explains the broad duties of the Levites this way: "They performed, not only the rites of religion, but also the duties of all those offices of state, for which learning was necessary. They were by birth devoted to the cultivation of the sciences, especially the science of government and jurisprudence. They were to study the book of the law; to make, preserve, and disseminate correct copies of it; to instruct the people both in human and divine learning; to test the accuracy of weights and measures; to exhort the soldiers, and inspire them with courage, when about to engage in battle; to perform the duty of police physicians; to determine and announce the moveable feasts, new moons and intercalary years; to discharge the functions of judges and genealogist; with a variety of other duties. (Numb. 18:2-; Lev. 25:8-9; Deut. 17:9; 31:11-13; Lev. 13:14; 1 Chron. 23:4; 2 Chron. 17:7-9; 19:8; 34:13; Mal. 2:7)

[98] Wines, p. 232.

[99] Wines, p. 235.

[100] See the books *Watchmen on the Walls* and *America's Providential History*, published by the Providence Foundation.

[101] Wines, p. 247.

[102] Some may ask, if the Hebrew form of government was divine, why did it not remain? If men had been more perfect it would have stood forever, but men (and certainly the Israelites under the Old Covenant) are sinful and their passions are corrupted. Israel fell beneath the weight of its own vices. Divine power operating in the heart of man is necessary to support divine government.

[103] *Our Ageless Constitution*, edited by W. David Stedman and LaVaughn G. Lewis, Asheboro, NC, 1987, p. 32.

[104] "On the Cod Fishery Bill, granting Bounties," February 7, 1792, in *The Debates of the Several State Conventions on the Adoption of the Federal Constitution as Recommended by the General Convention at Philadelphia in 1787, in Five Volumes*, by Jonathan Elliot, New York: Burt Franklin R, Vol. IV, p. 429.

[105] Thomas Jefferson, "The Kentucky Resolutions of 1798," *The Annals of America, Vol. 4*, Chicago: Encyclopedia Britannica, Inc., 1976, p. 66.

[106] Andrew W. Young, *First Lessons in Civil Government*, Auburn, N.Y.: H. and J.C. Ivison, 1846, p. 16.

[107] English historian Lord Action (1843-1902) wrote in 1881: "All power tends to corrupt and absolute power corrupts absolutely."

[108] Baron De Montesquieu, *The Spirit of Laws*, quoted in *Christian History of the Constitution*, Verna Hall, Foundation for American Christian Education, pp. 134-135.

[109] For more on this see Stephen McDowell and John McDowell, "We the People, or We the Judges," https://providencefoundation.com/we-the-people-or-we-the-judges/

[110] See *Defensive War in a Just Cause Sinless, A Sermon, Preached on the Day of the Continental Fast, 1775*, by Rev. David Jones, in *America's Providential History, A Documentary Sourcebook*, edited by Stephen McDowell, Charlottesville: Providence Foundation, 2010, p. 46.

[111] Thomas Jefferson, "Inauguration Address, March 4, 1801," *The Writings of Thomas Jefferson*, Washington, DC: The Thomas Jefferson Memorial Association, 1903, 3:321.

[112] https://providencefoundation.com/christian-ideas-in-the-declaration-of-independence/

[113] Baron De Montesquieu, *The Spirit of Laws*, translated from the French by Thomas Nugent, 2 Vols., New York: the Colonial Press, 1899, Vol. 2, p. 27.

[114] Ibid., pp. 29-30.

[115] *Sources of Our Liberties*, Richard L. Perry, editor, American Bar Foundation, 1952, p. 211.

[116] Intercessors for America offers many great prayer resources including the booklet, "Praying for the Government Prayer Guide," see: https://www.ifapray.org/resources/prayer-guides-and-resources/

[117] Gary DeMar, *God and Government, Vol. 2, Issues in Biblical Perspective*, Atlanta, 1984, pp. 131, 121.

[118] David Chilton, *Productive Christians in an Age of Guilt Manipulators: A Biblical Response to Ronald J. Sider*, Tyler, Tex.: Institute for Christian Economics, 1982, p. 63.

[119] For more on this subject see, Edward A. Powell and Rousas John Rushdoony, *Tithing and Dominion*, Vallecito, Cal.: Ross House Books, 1979.

[120] Letter to David McClure, October 25, 1836, *Letters of Noah Webster*, Harry R. Warfel editor, New York: Library Publishers, 1953, p, 453.

[121] Mary-Elaine Swanson, *The Education of James Madison, A Model for Today*, Montgomery: The Hoffman Education Center for the Family, 1992, p. 53.

[122] John Witherspoon, "The Dominion of Providence over the Passions of Men. A Sermon Preached at Princeton on the 17th of May, 1776," in *Political Sermons of the American Founding Era, 1730-1805*, edited by Ellis Sandoz, Indianapolis: Liberty Press, 1991, p. 557-558.

[123] John Wingate Thorton, *The Pulpit of the American Revolution: or, the Political Sermons of the Period of 1776*, Boston: Gould and Lincoln, 1860, p. XXXVIII.

[124] Quoted in Charles Hull Wolfe, *Three Churches, One Nation*, an unpublished manual.

[125] *The Book of Abigail and John, Selected Letters of the Adams Family, 1762-1784*, Edited by L.H. Butterfield, Marc Friedlaender, and Mary-Jo Kline, Cambridge, Mass.: Harvard University Press, 1975, p. 129.

[126] J.T. Headley, *The Chaplains and Clergy of the Revolution*, republished by 20th Century Reformation Hour, 1976 (originally published by Charles Scribner, New York, in 1864), p. 101.

[127] Ibid.

[128] Alice Baldwin, *The New England Clergy and the American Revolution*, Fredick Ungar Pub. Co., 1928.

[129] See Beliles and McDowell, *America's Providential History*.

[130] To learn about some of these men, as well as many other significant Christians, see Stephen McDowell, *Transforming Nations through Biblical Work*, Charlottesville: Providence Foundation, 2018.

[131] John Wingate Thorton, *The Pulpit of the American Revolution: or, the Political Sermons of the Period of 1776*, Boston: Gould and Lincoln, 1860, p. XXII, XXIII, XXVI.

[132] W. DeLoss Love, Jr., *The Fast and Thanksgiving Days of New England*, New York: Houghton, Mifflin and Co., 1895, p. 41.

[133] Love, *The Fast and Thanksgiving Days of New England*. Love lists the days of fasting and thanksgiving. He also lists 622 fast and thanksgiving day sermons that were published, dating from 1636 to 1815.

[134] Catherine Drinker Bowen, *John Adams and the American Revolution*, New York: Grosset & Dunlap, 1950, p. 10-12.

[135] B.F. Morris, pp 530-531.

[136] Ibid.

[137] See Mark A. Beliles and Stephen K. McDowell, *America's Providential History*, Charlottesville, VA: Providence Foundation, 1989, p. 141, and Peter Force, *American Archives: A Documentary History of the English Colonies in North America, Fourth Series*, Washington: M. St. Clair and Peter Force, 1846, pp. 1278, 1471.

[138] The Virginia Gazette, Nov. 20, 1779, Number 4, Williamsburg: Printed by Dixon & Nicolson.

[139] Benjamin F. Morris, *Christian Life and Character of the Civil Institutions of the United States*, Powder Springs, GA: American Vision, 2007 (reprint of 1864 edition), pp. 675-678. See W. DeLoss Love, *The Fast and Thanksgiving Days of New England* for an extensive list of government proclamations for Days of Prayer.

[140] See *A Compilation of the Messages of the Presidents*, James D. Richardson, ed., New York: Bureau of National Literature, 1897.

[141] For examples of some of these public sermons see: *Political Sermons of the American Founding Era, 1730-1805*, Ellis Sandoz, editor, Indianapolis: Liberty Press, 1991. John Wingate Thorton, *The Pulpit of the American Revolution: or, the Political Sermons of the Period of 1776*, Boston: Gould and Lincoln, 1860.

[142] Charles G. Finney, *Revivals of Religion*, Virginia Beach: CBN University Press, 1978, pp. 311-312.

[143] *Eerdmans' Handbook to the Bible*, edited by David Alexander and Pat Alexander, Grand Rapids, 1973, p. 588.

[144] To read about some of these individuals see Stephen McDowell, *Transforming Nations Through Biblical Work*.

[145] William Jay, *The Life of John Jay*, New York: J. & J. Harper, 1833, Vol. II, p. 376, Letter to John Murray, Jr. on October 12, 1816.

[146] For more on Moses and the unique government of the Hebrew Republic, see Chapter 8.

[147] Matthias Burnet, "Religion and Government the Foundations of Order, Peace, and Security, in Society," An Election Sermon Preached at a General Assembly of the State of Connecticut at Hartford, on the Day of the Anniversary Election, May 12, 1803.

[148] For a biblical approach to assisting the poor see George Grant, *In the Shadow of Plenty*.

[149] See Chapters 7 and 9.

[150] Matthias Burnet.

[151] Chandler Robbins, "And Also in Judah Things Went Well." A Sermon Preached before His Excellency John Hancock, Governour; His Honor Samuel Adams, Lieutant-Governour; the Honourable the Council, and the Honourable the Senate and House of Representatives, of the Commonwealth of Massachusetts, May 25, 1791, Being the Day of General Election.

[152] Daniel Shute, *An Election Sermon*, Boston, 1768, "Why government needs a constitution and what should be in it." *American Political Writing during the Founding Era, 1760-1805*, Vol. 1, Charles S. Hyneman, Donald S. Lutz, Indianapolis: Liberty Press, 1983, p. 124.

[153] Ibid.

[154] Chandler Robbins.

[155] "Circular to the Governors of the States," June 8, 1783, *The Writings of George Washington from the Original Manuscript Sources, 1745-1799*, edited by John C. Fitzpatrick, Washington: U.S. Government Printing Office, 1931, Vol. 26, p. 496.

[156] See Stephen McDowell, *Apostle of Liberty: the World-Changing Leadership of George Washington*, Nashville: Cumberland House, 2007, pp. 166-167. See also Stephen McDowell and Mark Beliles, *In God We Trust Tour Guide*, pp. 70-71.

[157] Matthias Burnet.

[158] Matthias Burnet.

[159] Chandler Robbins.

[160] Noah Webster, *History of the United Sates*, New Haven: Durrie & Peck, 1833, pp. 307-308.

[161] Wines, p. 7.

[162] Benjamin Rush, *Essays, Literary, Moral and Philosophical*, Philadelphia: printed by Thomas and William Bradford, 1806, p.93.

Made in USA - North Chelmsford, MA
1057740_9781887456586
03.20.2020 0031